The Leader's Voice

Second Edition

*How your communication
can inspire action
and get results!*

RON CROSSLAND

SelectBooks, Inc.

New York

This edition published by SelectBooks, Inc.
For information address SelectBooks, Inc., New York, New York.

Second Edition

ISBN 978-1-59079-152-3

Library of Congress Cataloging-in-Publication Data

Crossland, Ron.
The leader's voice / Ron Crossland. -- 2nd ed.
p. cm.
Rev. ed. of: The leader's voice / [Boyd] Clarke & [Ron] Crossland. 1st ed.
c2002.
Includes bibliographical references and index.
ISBN 978-1-59079-152-3 (hardbound : alk. paper)
1. Leadership. 2. Communication in organizations. 3. Interpersonal
communication. I. Clarke, Boyd. Leader's voice. II. Title.

HD57.7.C5386 2008
658.4'5--dc22

2008000731

Manufactured in the United States of America

10 9 8 7 6 5 4 3 2 1

I dedicate this book to Boyd Clarke,
my longtime friend and business partner.
Your work lives on in the lives of the many you touched, Boyd.

CONTENTS

PREFACE

G o see the cherry trees blossoming in Washington, D.C., sometime if you can. I once saw them on a bright, cool spring day with my late business partner, Boyd Clarke. Our conversation felt as crisp and alive as the air and blooms that spread a canopy over our intense conversation. We did not realize it then, but this moment marked a change in the direction of our careers.

Boyd and I had just visited John W. Gardner for the third time. Students of leadership are familiar with Gardner's book *On Leadership*, but it was his earlier works, *Excellence* and *Self-Renewal*, that established his voice in the arena of civic reform and individual excellence. Gardner had a varied and illustrative career that included writing, psychological assessment and personnel deployment for the Office of Strategic Services during World War II, leading the Carnegie Corporation, working as secretary of the U.S. Department of Health, Education, and Welfare under president Lyndon Johnson, launching Common Cause and the Independent Sector, and teaching at his alma mater, Stanford University.

Gardner was a busy and important man. I remember wishing I had an office like his—ceiling-to-floor bookshelves, huge windows that illuminated everything, and an aircraft-carrier-size desk. It was a working scholar and activist's intellectual base. Boyd and I had called Gardner during our tenure at AT&T. We didn't know him personally—we probably had a full six degrees of separation from him at the time—but we had developed a large appetite for leadership during the post-telecommunication deregulation days that changed how U.S. citizens would experience voice and data exchanges. This passion for leadership helped us take a number of risks.

We had been trying to arrange a skip-level meeting with our boss's boss to talk about our leadership development plans for AT&T, but our upper management was far too involved in the rolling waves of uncertainty that kept AT&T in rough seas for more than a decade after 1984. Our management had no time for leadership development, as they were grappling with finding new strategic direction and downsizing a workforce. The irony of the situation was frustrating.

Boyd and I were planning on leaving AT&T to start our own consulting company and thought Gardner might advise us on the enterprise. So we were quite pleased when Gardner made time for us and devoted his full attention to our plans. We had developed a rapport with him and were looking for his guidance on how to proceed. Toward the end of the conversation, Boyd asked, "John, what is the most important aspect of leadership in your opinion?"

Gardner did not lean back in reflection, but instead leaned forward with enthusiasm. He said, "Communication. Communication between leaders and constituents is at the heart of everything."

We conversed on this topic for a little while with Gardner and then left his office and found ourselves strolling beside the cherry trees, enjoying the promise of renewal that spring often stimulates. I have always felt that the certainty of Gardner's response was a conviction he had developed while being a leader himself, rather than just from philosophic or research bias. It was his conviction that pushed Boyd and me to tumble his perspective around in our minds. (Gardner was always getting people to consider his perspectives; while serving as president of the Carnegie Foundation, he encouraged Lyndon Johnson to start the Whitehouse Fellowship program.) Frankly, we were excited and skeptical about the power of his statement. Over the course of our walk we decided we would start researching leadership communication and see what would happen.

This decision developed into a long-term love affair with communication. The second edition of this book is the latest expression of that devotion to understand what Gardner suggested was at the heart of everything. The organization of this edition is different from the first one. It leans more in the direction of research and explanation than the first. It updates our thesis in the light of new ideas that have developed since 2002. It also provides more practical ideas about how to develop your voice than the first edition.

John Gardner passed away in 2002 at the ripe age of eighty-nine. Three years later my friend and business partner of more than twenty years, Boyd Clarke, passed away at the far too tender age of fifty-two. I hope this edition honors their voices.

ACKNOWLEDGMENTS

A book has many voices. At least it is produced with many voices, some revealed in the writing, some that influence the book's production, and some that inspire the writer.

The voices of my colleagues at Bluepoint Leadership Development are echoed in the pages. They are a band of hard-working professionals who arise each day to change the world through accelerating the supply and development of leaders throughout the world. Their collective thoughts can be recognized here—in some cases there's likely a phrase or two that can be attributed to particular individuals.

Jill Hughes editing work is not just superb, in my opinion it is perfect. Her copyediting skills are enviable and her occasional suggestions concerning confusing passages helped me make my point more clearly. I've learned not to argue with her concerning matters of editing, as I only reveal my lesser understanding. I hear, tremble, and obey.

Andrew Newman's voice is all over the jacket cover. Designing covers for anyone requires insight, a good eye, and patience. I appreciate his work and professionalism.

There are a number of scholars, researchers, and writers whose voices have bounced in my brain as I constructed this second edition. You will meet them in the pages that follow but I am truly grateful for their contributions to my understanding.

A book may owe its conception to the author, but its birth requires a publisher. I owe a great deal to the wisdom and care of Kenzi Sugihara and his fine staff at SelectBooks and for their contribution to the completion of this project. No one asks me to hurry up and finish with as much kindness and grace as Kenzi. His requests feel more like wind in my sails than a kick in the butt.

Susan, Corbin, and Jonathan tease me about a condition they have long accepted. Often at dinner or when we as a family are driving around town, they will ask me a question and get the "hourglass response." You know the little hourglass that spins on your PC when the computer is busy and you momentarily have to wait while it is thinking? The hourglass evidently spins in front of my face as it sometimes takes two or three minutes for me to answer a question. Usually it is because I'm thinking about my writing and when I do that, everything else gets processed in the background. I want all three of them to know how grateful I am for their acceptance of my hourglass moments and for their encouragement and support of my writing.

INTRODUCTION

The Greek mathematician Archimedes discovered how to move the whole earth. All he needed was a lever long enough and a place to stand. The task of uniting a business and moving it forward can seem as simple in principle but as difficult in reality as Archimedes's claim. The ability to communicate powerfully is one of the great levers leaders need, and credibility is their place to stand. Unfortunately, leaders often shorten the lever through over-attention to a single aspect of communication (as you'll see outlined in chapter 7). And they can lose their solid place to stand as their credibility becomes loose, slippery, perhaps even turning to quicksand.

Failing to create the organizational focus, commitment, and energy necessary to "move the whole organization" is a common problem. As Claudio Fernández-Aráoz, Buenos Aires business and operations manager for the highly regarded executive search and talent management firm Egon Zehnder International, suggests, "The CEOs and senior executives of Enron Corporation, WorldCom Inc., and other disgraced companies have certainly gotten their fair share of press, but the huge scandal that nobody talks about is the multitude of cases in which top positions are filled with mediocre people."[1]

Chapter 1 of this edition of *The Leader's Voice* will address part of the problem of mediocre leaders by examining communication competency. Among the issues this chapter will cover are remedies for four unconscious, automatic assumptions most leaders make that leave their communication mediocre or worse. These four fatal assumptions are:

1. Constituents UNDERSTAND what was communicated.

2. Constituents AGREE with what was communicated.

3. Constituents CARE about what was communicated.

4. Constituents will take APPROPRIATE ACTION.

We agree with the perspective of Nobel laureate George Bernard Shaw, who once said, "The single biggest problem in communication is the illusion that it has taken place."[2] (He also provided us with the often-used quote "He who can, does. He who cannot, teaches."[3] This quote indicates why Boyd was an entrepreneur and Ron is a teacher.) Some of this illusion derives from the four fatal assumptions. Some arises because leaders attempt to master the techniques of communication rather than its essential principles.

This edition will help you to master those principles. Technique can amplify but not replace true voice. While many techniques are initially absorbed as imitations of others, they work well only when they become a natural part of your repertoire. Imitation can be an effective method to learn the craft of communication, but it does nothing for the character of the communicator. And most imitation, or platform skills, simply polish surface issues rather than explore deeper communication processes.

Chapter 1 will focus on communication research. It will help illustrate how we derived our model of facts, emotions, and symbols. Chapter 2 reviews modern neurobiology that explains why this model works. Those who are less interested in such background may choose to bypass this chapter, but please at least scan it to get a sense of the basics. It provides a thesis for the rest of the book, using a "central movie" metaphor. Understanding why and how this metaphor is used will help make the rest of the reading understandable. Many readers will find this chapter one of the most interesting, as it may alter your perception of how brain systems and communication work—at least as we understand it so far.

Chapter 3 discusses how to develop a key message, or central movie. The idea of key messages applies to nearly all non-logistical communication. Logistical communication has to do with basic concepts like when and where to meet, who to invite, what the meeting is about, and other issues related to the details of a project, meeting, or situation. All other communication, whether provided orally in a face-to-face situation, or through written communication such as email or instant messaging, can benefit from the power of developing a central movie.

Chapter 4 consists of two case studies. One involves the developmental years of one of the most successful niche retailers in North America, LensCrafters, before and just after it became part of the Luxottica Retail Group. The other case is about one of the most prosperous cable networks, TNT.

The next three chapters will deal directly with the three channels of communication: factual, emotional, and symbolic. They are presented in their order of difficulty for most communicators. Symbolic communication requires the most development for most managers, followed by emotional, and then factual. Although this order may not represent your own strengths, it does reflect the general trend.

Chapter 8 deals with the three aspects or competencies of leadership that can cause a highly effective communicator to lose his or her voice. Each of these competencies are not about communication but rather leadership aspects that can mute or destroy your ability to be heard. These ideas are critical to leadership communication. The three channels of communication appear to be generally true for all communicators, regardless of role. However, communication is baked with other competencies in the leadership role.

One Voice

We believe that one voice can make all the difference. One voice will be heard above the clamor of the crowd, above the noise of the street, and above the stampede in the market. When we hear it, we respond. It resonates with our best intentions and aspirations. Like the bellows of a blacksmith, it fans the flames of desire to rise above the mundane and make a mark. It encourages us to do great work, to be extraordinary. It energizes and unites.

It is The Leader's Voice.

This voice simplifies the complex and clarifies the cloudy. It quiets dissonance and strikes the chord that defines direction. It replaces despair with hope, and cynicism with purpose. It plainly states the unspoken, describes precisely what people feel but fear to say, and calls others to action when they are paralyzed. The genius of leadership is to speak with a voice that pushes past cynicism, doubt, and uncertainty.

The Leader's Voice allows you to speak the truth so that others can distinguish it from spin. It establishes a compelling context while others squabble over trivial content. It challenges others to take a stand before certainty arrives. It is authentically your voice. Even when your words feel clumsy, your voice is eloquent. When your passion declares the direction you will go, it unites those who will follow and divides those who will not.

If you choose to lead, prepare to take a stand. It is not for the fainthearted. Some will judge you unfairly, blaming you for their lack of success. Others will expect resources you cannot give, answers you do not have, and permission you cannot grant. You will be misquoted. Your judgment will be questioned.

You will certainly stumble. Failure will stalk you like a predator. The toughest problems will be yours alone. You must take responsibility for the failures and give credit for the successes. Lose the fantasy that you will be cherished, immortalized, or revered. Expect long hours and few moments of gratitude.

Expect also to soar beyond your expectations. Constituents will create magic inspired by your voice. They will make you glad you chose to lead. They will hear what you say, understand it, care about it, and act with a gusto that will amaze. Together, you and your constituents will engage in the best work of your lives.

The heart of the matter for business leaders is to communicate so compellingly as to raise the consciousness, conviction, and competence of your constituency. We hope this slim volume will aid you in this quest.

1

THE CASE FOR COMMUNICATION

O f all the chapters in this book, this one was the easiest to write. At one time I lost this chapter before backing it up (the phrase "not knowing whether to laugh or cry" went to a whole new level for me when I discovered the loss), but I found that rewriting it, while irritating, was easy. The reason is simple—leaders have been beached by a tsunami of data over the past twenty years with regard to the need for increasing their leadership communication effectiveness. Before we revisit a few cupfuls from this overwhelming wave of data, however, consider the two scenes depicted below.

Scene 1. Acrobatic entertainers powerbock around the ballroom, their spring-loaded locomotion vaulting them at times to dizzying heights as the loud, energetic music cranks up the noise to construction-site levels. Banners announcing this year's kickoff theme dance across the plasma screens, alternating with vivid candid photos of various attendees. The fanfare fades as a key executive is introduced. After an initial big smile and obligatory joke, the lights dim, the projectors beam, and you settle back for another mesmerizing slide show. A barrage of multicolored charts, graphs, and statistics swarm across your eyes as the executive's voice becomes more monotonic, less engaging, like chewing gum long after the flavor is gone.

It's not just the carefully scripted words of a person being politically correct, legally sanitized, and emotionally flat that begins to hypnotize, but you start to recognize this presentation as a recital of

5

facts you already know, with more effort applied to the slides than to the message. Hoping you may still gain some insight, some value from this recitation, you wish you could access your email—or you actually do pull it up on your favorite handheld device. You keep one ear tuned for any bits of new information, but you struggle with boredom, wishing you could employ your time elsewhere.

During the awkward silence following the executive's request for questions, you realize you do have questions but don't care enough to ask them. Most befuddling of all, you still are not clear about the message. You can recall this year's theme when prompted, but you don't know how it connects to your company's overall mission. You recall the familiar facts, but you are fuzzy about the company's goals. The leader concludes to polite applause and during the subsequent cocktail hour receives the obligatory confirmation that it was one of the best presentations of the day, which may be sad but true.

Scene 2. The auditorium lights dim to the stirring sounds of Olympic trumpets. The inspirational video begins, highlighting the accomplishments of humankind and your division. You are feeling positive, uplifted, and even the most cynical in the audience feel proud. The executive takes the stage to loud applause. This time there are no slides and no notes. Speaking with a dynamic, sincere voice, he recounts the inspiring story of the salesperson who went to extraordinary efforts to land the huge account. He describes in humorous detail what the vice president of International Development had to eat while striking a new business deal in China. And he reminds everyone of the above-the-call-of-duty story of the customer service efforts in the company's new Latin America office.

The inspirational value of the message is high. You leave feeling alert and excited, but you still don't know what vital action to take for your company. You can sing the company's anthem and even like the tune. But after the presentation is over you realize that although it feels good to be part of this company, you are uncertain about the strategy or how your team can help execute it. In fact, you realize that while you are inspired by the moving stories, you wonder if any of your team's work will produce such results, since your team is at a crossroads in choosing its direction. You've been seeking information that will help you decide, and you realize that the kickoff meeting really didn't help.

SCENE 3. You stumble to work, weary from the weeklong business trip that was necessary but now feels like it just backed you up two or three days. You did your best to stay on top of things, but your unanswered email is nearing an all-time high and you have some messages that require your immediate attention (or so they claim). But this is the first Monday of the month and time to attend your boss's monthly meeting. As you drop your bag and try to reacquaint yourself with where stuff is in your office, you begin an internal debate. On the one hand you tell yourself that missing the meeting could be a politically damaging move, but on the other hand you remind yourself that these meetings rarely accomplish anything. Your boss is not particularly effective at running the show, and decisions often appear arbitrary and are communicated in a rather heavy-handed manner. Speaking up to the boss or trying to spark a dialogue usually doesn't overturn things, and today you don't even have the energy to try. You glance at the time and realize you have to decide right now about attending the meeting.

A Long Look at Communication Effectiveness

These three scenes may feel familiar to you. Even if they don't, you can probably create others from memory of well-intentioned or dictatorial leaders whose communication effectiveness was not particularly great. Everyone feels that time has become shorter and that having the time to prepare for effective communication is nonexistent. Managers want to get information out clearly, effectively, and fast. Managers may believe they have smart people who know what to do. Or they may believe that time pressures demand that they simply tell others what to do rather than engage them in other ways, because they aren't going to get the message anyway. Organizations have Web sites and internal communications teams working overtime to remind people of missions, goals, and values. And you realize as you compose emails in your mind that this passage from *Made to Stick* certainly applies to your situation: "In all likelihood your process-improvement memo will not circulate decades from now as a proverb in another culture."[1] So why bother to work too hard at this routine message?

These pressures, despite their reality, do not relieve you as a leader from your communication responsibility. You may have taken courses on presentation skills or business writing skills, and you may really try hard, but you may still remain relatively average in your ability to communicate. The underlying problems with ineffective communication have been researched and documented over a long period of time. In each decade from roughly the 1940s, the same problems have been catalogued, and occasionally some new perspective has been developed to aid leaders in their communication. Most of these were regurgitations of basic rhetorical principles. Some were departures from traditional rhetorical ideas and proposed new ways of thinking about communication in general. Some included the neurological underpinnings of communication as an aid to understanding how the best leaders communicate so well.

Leaping with gusto into this tsunami allowed Boyd and me to renew our friendship with communication and reconsider what the old and new constructs were suggesting. For the past twenty years the facts concerning leadership communication have changed little. But knowing what to do about it has changed a great deal as some older theories and practices have been replaced by new evidence. The following selections from this vast wave of data are representative of hundreds just like them. We provide them so that you can surf the territory quickly and thoroughly.

Twenty Years of Research

In 1986, as Boyd and I met with John Gardner, we pored over all the secondary research data we could find on leadership communication.

One typical research report at the time showed that in detailed interviews with 246 senior executives, more than 90 percent of them felt they were above average in their communication abilities. In fact, nearly half of them felt they communicated very effectively.[2] Yet other reports were showing that communication ineffectiveness was at an all-time high, especially in the arena of communicating vision and strategy. This dichotomy was confirmed by our own research. We found that roughly 90 percent of leaders gave themselves a better than average score at communicating, but roughly only 30 percent of constituents felt their managers were able to effectively communicate vision.[3] One international study from this era showed that most senior executives not only believed conveying a strong sense of the future was the number one most needed and number one most deficient competency facing next-generation leaders, but also that communication was the primary skill required to excite others.

Because the late 1980s and early 1990s were the age of vision, much of the research regarding leadership communication was heavily influenced by how vision and strategy were communicated. By 1999, however, communication and engagement became the focus. The Gallup Management Group examined their database of employee exit interviews and created one of the most often repeated statistics of all time. Their analysis showed that 71 percent of workers quit their jobs because of their direct boss.[4] This single datum sparked a widespread renewal of interest in employee engagement. Yet during this time similar analyses by other groups conducting similar research in Europe as well as in the United States showed that the number one difficulty leaders were having that prompted employees to quit was their boss's poor communication abilities.[5]

By the turn of the millennium this connection between leadership communication, vision, and engagement became more pronounced and more refined. Our research in 2002 of 1,104 business professionals, while we were with Tom Peters Company, indicated that 86 percent of executives felt they were effective communicators, but only 17 percent of their constituents believed their managers were effective communicators.[6] The gap had widened. Towers Perrin research underscored this trend. They showed that 61 percent of what impacts behavior in organizations can be traced to the "personal voice" of the leader, which carried more weight than the more disembodied voice of the organization, referred to as the "institutional voice."[7]

In 2003 research from the United Kingdom indicated that these problems were suffered at board levels as well as throughout the ranks. One study indicated that 85 percent of constituents believed their executives needed to improve their communication skills, and only 10 percent believed executives could deliver messages effectively. Charles Wace, CEO of U.K. media giant the Twofour Group, stated the obvious—"There is a growing body of evidence that supports the importance of effective corporate communications"—as he discussed the weight of these statistics in light of the role communication plays in impacting brand image, employee engagement, and even share price. Wayne Drew, CEO of the International Visual Communications Association, also remarked, "At present it seems board members are lacking the confidence and skills enabling them to talk to staff effectively."[8]

A 2005 study by the International Association of Business Communicators and Right Management Consultants showed that only one-third of 472 companies surveyed were "successful in motivating employees to understand, be committed to, and carry out their employer's business strategy in their daily jobs." The top reasons cited for the other two-thirds' inability to get these basic jobs done were inconsistent messages, lack of leader visibility—especially during tough times—and a lack of employees' trust in leadership. Nearly two-thirds of these companies had stated that their number one communications goal was to align people to the corporate strategy, yet only slightly more than a third believed they had been successful in such efforts. Paul Sanchez, chair of the IABC Research Foundation, remarked, "The daily struggles faced by internal communicators worldwide have largely been unaddressed."[9]

"The CEO gets too much agreement and too little candor, and this is the most frequent reason for a leadership intervention to help with strategic alignment, team building, or comparable exercise," said Christopher Rice, CEO of BlessingWhite. In an October 2007 report this company indicated the top seven chronic CEO complaints were:

- Getting too much agreement from staff.
- Hearing too much data and not enough insight from others.
- So much focus on competence that emotional energy for the work seemed drained.
- Lots of talk and little action to change.
- Constant communication without anyone "getting" the message.
- Talent departures without a true understanding of why.
- People feeling widespread change without seeing the big picture of why.[10]

These statements echo earlier work mentioned in Jim Shaffer's book *The Leadership Solution*. One of his clients said, "It can be very frustrating. It's like we say it, we say it, and we say it again, and people are just not hearing it. I know it's not their fault. But it's frustrating as hell when we can't connect."[11] Shaffer concluded that, and we would agree, "Confusion and misinformation aren't selective about where they infest a business."[12]

A branch of linguistic philosophy that explores the everyday impact of communication is speech act theory. Early theorists were Adolf Reinach and John L. Austin, who both basically proposed the idea that by saying something, we do something. Contemporary theorists such as John Searle and Fernando Flores have furthered the field with their thinking and research. Fundamentally, the speech act theory suggests several important ideas. It suggests that speech acts commit a speaker to some factual truth, cause someone to take action, commit the speaker (and perhaps others) to future acts, reflect the speaker's emotional state about the content of the spoken words, or actually declare the conclusion of certain actions and what they mean, often in symbolic terms (think announcing the sales award winner as the customer service role model, declaring the launch of a new product as the wave of the future, or announcing a merger as a marriage made in heaven).

This method of studying the impact of language and ideas is making its way into managerial fields of communication, because managers spend perhaps two-thirds to three-fourths of their day in formal or informal discussions with coworkers, colleagues, customers, or other business parties. Business conversations are rife with speech acts—doing things by saying them. "Consciously or not, managers (through their utterances) create an intricate web of requests, commitments, assertions, and declarations that affect how people in their organizations act."[13]

Donald Sull and Charles Spinosa suggest that these speech acts help us understand the essence of execution by linking everyday communication with commitment. The better the communication, the stronger the commitment. Sull and Spinosa suggest that the structure of these communications stimulates the manner in which thousands of commitments affect strategy, engagement, and most other organizational outcomes. Terming these commitments as "promises," their research suggests that such promises are critical to business success but often fail in practice to produce the desired outcomes due to a breakdown in communication. "To a large extent, these breakdowns result from managers' and employees' imperfect understanding of how to make effective commitments."[14]

Sull and Spinosa go on to suggest five characteristics of a good promise. One of the five is central to the thesis of this book: good promises are mission based. They cite the following example:

> The U.S. Marine Corps, for instance, uses what it calls mission-based orders. These requests clearly articulate what the commanding officer wants and why, while leaving the methods of implementation to the discretion of the subordinate officer closest to the situation on the ground. Each order includes an explanation—known as the commander's intent—of why the objective matters to the commanding officer and to his superior as well. Business leaders can apply a similar discipline by explain-

ing to providers why requests matter to them. They can gauge whether providers understand and support the overall rationales for a request by asking them to articulate in their own words why the request matters.[15]

Three Common Communication Problems

This short skim across the communication tsunami illustrates the major themes of nearly all the research we've seen over the past twenty years. The nature of the complaints rarely changes, and while the remedies are worded in the fashionable terms of each decade, the advice doesn't change. Communication chronically emerges as a glaring problem for most organizations, and individual leaders' average or less communication skills are part of what contributes to disengagement, a loss of alignment, and a dissonance between leaders and constituents. In our humble opinion (supported by some research, of course), there are three consistent problems that correlate with this lackluster aggregate annual communication report card. These three chronic problems are:

1. Leaders believe they are above average at communicating, despite evidence to the contrary.

2. Leaders believe in the myth that more communication is needed. But it's not more, it's better communication that is required.

3. Leaders believe taking one or two short courses on communication is all they ever need to improve.

Most leaders we have worked with over the years are hardworking and well intentioned. Yet most are more willing to invest in almost any other competence, such as strategic thinking, business analysis, or other operational skills, long before they will invest in improving their communication skills. This is because most of us believe the communication problem lies elsewhere ("I'm better than average"). And if we do attend training, what we get is the same old stuff (which is good stuff, by the way, even if it does not provide the most complete picture of how superior communicators work their magic). This helps stimulate the conclusion for many leaders that they simply need to get out there and keep repeating themselves in the same inadequate ways.

We are not down on leaders who struggle with these issues. It is very understandable that our basic human nature biases most of us to believe we communicate better than we do, and that modern courses in communication have not yet caught up with modern understanding of how communication works. For example, take a look at how most communication training works.

Presentation and public speaking courses are imitation training. They focus on the face-to-face communication situations by teaching leaders to use strong gestures, smile, maintain good eye contact, and relate engaging stories, because these actions imitate what it appears great communicators are doing. It tells them to speak with active, lively language. Leaders are instructed to alter pitch, rhythm, and cadence. Connect with individuals in the audience—don't canvass. They are commanded to never turn their back on the audience and to never, ever place their hands in their pockets. Above all, avoid the dreaded "fig leaf maneuver." Don't pace! Tell them what you are going to tell them, tell them, and then tell them what you told them. Use humor, and be sure you are aware of social sensitivities when you do. And that's just for oral communication!

Written communication follows different rules and techniques. Most revolve around grammar, composition, and modern etiquette. Yet we still find that many email messages read like assembly directions for a backyard swing set, and others read like cryptic fortune cookies. Still others ramble on using informal language to try to convey a more casual and "real" voice, but the rambling is often confusing. Some corporate annual reports are stiffer than obituaries. In fact, many corporations have abandoned using annual reports to reach shareholders or other interested parties, because they were never read, and have switched to using straightforward SEC reporting. Maybe the former annual reports were simply SEC standards dressed up with mysterious photos, stories wrung through the marketing sanitation machine, and illegible graphics. Too many memos are indistinguishable from subpoenas. Too many meetings are skipped because they drain energy like an audit update rather than inject energy with enthusiasm and progress.

Public speaking and presentation skills training are great despite their focus on imitation. Imitation often doesn't explore the deeper principles of communication, but it can do a great job on how to polish the surface. Rhetorical study couldn't hurt, but often the terminology obscures the ideas. And as we will show in later chapters, rhetorical theory alone doesn't account for exactly how the best communicators work their magic.

As advisers, we often found ourselves in the communication wasteland between business leaders and their constituents. Business leaders, strategically positioned in their command posts, know where they are, who they want to communicate with, and what they want to say. Unfortunately, the troops hunkered down in the trenches never "get" the message. We have paid close attention to how business leaders attempt to communicate across this strangled divide, and we have gathered intelligence on the communication pattern that seems to make it through the fog of business.

We derived our ideas from the pattern we saw in our secondary research—the above-mentioned dozen or so studies are among eleven hundred or so we reviewed. We also conducted primary observation and coaching and found that the pattern of communication we hypothesized was at work was actually something we could coach and train. And finally, independent research studies, some testing our thesis and some from independent sources, have confirmed and are advancing our ideas.

Our research indicates that the best communicators, when they are at their best, use three channels of communication in all of their communication, from the big annual meetings to brief one-on-one conversations as they run through the airport. We also found that the most talented communicators can have their voices muted when any one of three leadership dimensions are compromised. The three channels of communication and the three dimensions of leadership that are critical to establishing and maintaining an effective leader's voice are:

Channels	*Dimensions*
Factual	Credibility
Emotional	Vision
Symbolic	Connection

Everyone uses all three channels, but most of us have developed an overreliance upon one or two and allow the other(s) to atrophy. This is like practicing only your swimming strokes when training for a triathlon. Others rely upon their strong credibility or clarity of vision but don't put much effort into using all three channels. However, even great communicators can lose a constituency if they lose credibility. When leaders lose credibility, we tend not to believe them, even if they seem to be the best of communicators. They lose their voice. Any leader who keeps a group lost in the fog too long will experience a loss of communication impact over time. Over time, if a leader cannot help complete the picture of the future and connect the strategy with the destination, constituents will tune out that person's voice. And those who lose connection with their constituents will not only find their voices muted, but those constituents will find ways of gaining attention, resources, and answers through other means, including making up their own stories about what is happening and believing in those stories more than they believe the leader.

So imagine encountering a leader with an average or less communication ability suffering a credibility, vision, or connection problem. You will see an environment in which poor promises are made, misunderstanding abounds, and engagement is low.

The Three Channels

Georgianne Smith completed one research effort that explored factual, emotional, and symbolic channels. She wanted to understand if using the three channels well distinguished good from better leaders.

She also wanted to see if the three channels would:

1. Increase overall communication effectiveness.
2. Increase the leader's ability to motivate others to take action.
3. Increase the leader's ability to influence a change of opinion or belief in others.

Smith created a number of hypotheses about the effect of the factual, emotional, and symbolic channels and how they would interact with credibility and vision. Her analyses reveal that six out of ten of her factors correlated strongly with the three outcomes above—overall effectiveness, motivating others to action, and influencing changes in opinion or belief. The six factors that emerged were emotions, facts, symbols, credibility, vision, and numbers. We were fascinated, but not surprised, that all the factors were important to communication and that the emotional factor was in a way the strongest of them all. While all the factors could be measured independently, they seemed to be interdependent in order to work the best. That is, they all worked together, except for one—numbers. Numbers alone (meaning the citation of explicit numerical data) was the weakest link in effectively communicating, motivating others, or influencing belief changes, and it did not play well with the other factors.[16]

In 2004 a group of fifteen researchers, representing the countries of China, France, India, Japan, the Netherlands, Singapore, Taiwan, Thailand, Turkey, and the United States, conducted an international study of managerial influence strategies upon social beliefs. They looked at the intersection of influence strategies, social beliefs, and cultural values. They wanted to understand if there was a general influence strategy that worked across many cultures or in a highly diverse culture. Specifically, they wanted to know the effect of three influence strategies—relationship-based, assertive, and persuasive—upon individual social beliefs, cultural values, and whether or not cultural values moderated the effect of the influence strategies upon individual beliefs.[17]

They defined a relationship-based strategy as one that includes giving gifts, inviting others to informal nonwork get-togethers, showcasing appropriate social small talk, and engaging in reciprocal exchanges (the influencer offers to repay the other person for the favor). Managers using this strategy attempt to use positive social skills to influence others to act. The assertive strategy consists of using repetitive pleas for help, using demands and threats to push others to help, or using the leverage of higher managerial support to gain attention to their request. Coercion is normally used as part of the assertive strategy. And the persuasive strategy includes using factual data along with an inspirational or emotional appeal in a request that helps the others see that what they will accomplish will have symbolic good for the group. The researchers found, "As expected, the mean ratings of influence strategies indicate that the persuasive strategy received the highest overall ratings of effectiveness across cultures."[18]

James Winchester took the thesis concerning facts, emotions, and symbols one step further. He wanted to find out if the factual and symbolic content of speeches from previous generations could still induce an emotional reaction from a diverse group of adults from a variety of work circumstances. He used the following speeches:

Martin Luther King, Jr. "I Have a Dream," 1963
John F. Kennedy, "Inaugural Address," 1961
Charles Lindbergh, "America First," 1941
Winston Churchill, "Their Finest Hour," 1940
Abraham Lincoln, "The Gettysburg Address," 1863
Sojourner Truth, "Ain't I a Woman?" 1851

Five out of six of these speeches were known to have had dramatic effects at the time of their oration. The Lindbergh speech is not generally considered to be of the same caliber as the others, having had little if any social impact during its day, and was used by Winchester as a counterbalance to the other five.

Winchester found that all but the Lindbergh speech produced qualitatively measurable emotional reactions from those who reread the speeches, even though some were originally delivered more than a century earlier. He further found that all the readers, whether politicians, business people, or clergy, saw that each of the original voices used the three channels that lead to an emotional reaction, but that *each voice was distinctly unique.* Winchester himself was so moved by the reaction of the group that his dissertation ends with these compelling thoughts: "Here is the central mystery of leadership communication, and through it humanity is directed to the most fundamental questions of existence. What are we? Why are we? And by what obscure and ancient mechanism do we touch so closely the lives, thoughts, and deeds of others with this sacred transubstantiation called human speech?"[19]

Conclusions

Leadership communication at its best (using facts, emotions, and symbols) establishes understanding, invites agreement, encourages and enables a willingness to act, and creates a path for action. Detailed data alone works like chloroform. Scintillating stories alone work like nitrous oxide. Emotional appeals alone work like energy drinks. All three channels working together can create the best communication, but a lack of credibility, a veil over vision, or a loss of connection can mute the voice of any great communicator.

It appears from the research leadership that communication problems are common and commonly persist. It also appears from the data that the way for any leader to upgrade his or her communication competence is to keep in mind the three channels of communication and three dimensions of leadership behavior. As Howard Gardner points out, yoking communication intelligence to personal intelligence can create the possibility for superior leadership.[20]

2

YOUR BRAIN ON COMMUNICATION

Over the past two decades, scientists have learned more about the human brain than they did in all of the prior two centuries. This pace of research has made it nearly impossible to remain current in the field. Some researchers estimate that 75 percent of what we know about the brain has been learned since 1990. As the brain's complexity has unraveled, scientists have been able to both extend and refine previous theories of the mind. Perhaps more important, there has been a revolution in the theories of how the complex structures and pathways of the brain do all the amazing work of providing humans with memory, reason, consciousness, our basic senses, our various intelligences from math to music to athletics, and body regulation. Left brain/right brain models or even the triune brain model have been modified, or replaced, with a more complete picture of how 100 billion neurons do their work. Each neuron connects to as many as ten thousand other neurons, which means the number of different points of contact in the brain is on the order of 1012 or so—more points of connection than the World Wide Web, and much faster, complex, and adaptable.

For many years Boyd and I knew that communicating in a combination of facts, emotions, and symbols worked, but we didn't always completely understand why. It was only after studying neurology that we understood the brain's role in communication. During all moments of consciousness the brain is trying to make sense and meaning of the world. It is vital to understand that the human brain is comprised of a variety of powerful systems, each of which play an irreplaceable role in this process. A person will generate explanations of what is happening that often defy the facts, distort emotional intensity, or miss the meaning of a situation altogether rather than live without an explanation. And we found that leaders who provide information that satisfies these systems are considered more powerful communicators than leaders who either don't do so or don't do so very well.

It appears there are numerous brain systems that affect factual, emotional, and symbolic communication. These are not the only systems in the brain. Some systems are devoted strictly to the senses, like, for example, how the eye's lens, retina, and the so-called visual cortex interact to provide our sense of sight. But many of our neurological systems are involved in supporting the factual, emotional, and symbolic pattern we documented. The neurological systems outlined in this chapter help us understand why we found what we found in our research. To get a basic understanding of these systems, please consider the following three case studies.

Factual System

The following account is perhaps the most well known, most often repeated Ripley's-Believe-It-Or-Not kind of story about the brain. Its familiarity still instructs. Phineas P. Gage had a mind-altering experience during the summer of 1848. A dynamic, young construction foreman for the Rutland & Burlington Railroad, he was admired by his colleagues and respected by his crew. Bright, likable, and experienced, he worked tirelessly and thoughtfully at a demanding job.

One day Phineas and his gang were clearing the right-of-way along the Black River near the town of Cavendish, Vermont. Taking responsibility for one of the more dangerous tasks, he prepared blasting holes for detonation by tamping gunpowder into holes in the area's rocky outcrops with a specially designed meter-long iron rod. It was a task that required concentration and precision.

One day, as he was pounding gunpowder with his iron rod, Phineas slipped. The strike ignited the powder, and the explosion rocketed the iron rod through his left cheek, his left eye, and the top of his head. It whistled through the air and landed dozens of yards away. Thrown to the ground by the blast, he was stunned and silent but fully awake. His men immediately rushed him to the local town doctor, who was amazed to see the railroad foreman alive. Phineas suffered a mild infection, some short-lived fevers, and lost his left eye. Within two months he was released from the doctor's care. It was a miracle.

After some time off, Phineas, still physically capable, tried to return to work. Tests indicated that his memory was intact. He could still count and complete other basic tasks. However, it soon became evident that his personality had permanently changed. He became fitful, irreverent, profane, impatient, obstinate, and indifferent to his fellow human beings. He became stuck in a cycle of flitting from one plan to another, never following through. His emotional energy was high, untamed, and often uncontrolled. His behavior changed so radically that some former friends had trouble even recognizing him. Though still physically competent, the railroad let him go because of his dramatic character change. Friends who knew the before-and-after Phineas said, "Gage was no longer Gage." From gaucho, to stagecoach driver, to circus freak, he held many jobs, holding none of them long. At the age of thirty-eight, he lapsed into a coma and died.

What happened to Phineas Gage has inspired scientists to consider many specific ideas about his transformation, but all the speculations agree on a major point: the system of the brain that was removed by the rod is a critical part of the logical system, the part of the brain associated with logical reasoning. This loss was substantiated by a wonderful reexamination of Gage's skull, conducted by Hanna Damasio and Albert Galaburda, that revealed with some precision which parts of the brain were removed.[1] Their analysis helped

Antonio Damasio to conclude that the loss Gage suffered eliminated a great deal of the cooperation between the brain's logical system and emotional system. This loss dramatically altered Gage's ability to reason well, to make plans for the future, to stay committed to any course of action for any appreciable length of time, and to function well socially. His brain's ability to make sense and meaning was altered permanently, and the effects of this played out for the remainder of his unfortunate life.

Emotional System

Antonio Damasio is not only a well-regarded doctor and neurologist but also a gifted writer, who brings complex scientific information to life with terrific stories. One of these, concerning a patient he refers to as Elliot, demonstrates how sense and meaning are altered when a part of the emotional system is lost.

Elliot had developed a tumor that altered his ability to function in the world. The tumor had not affected his better-than-average intellect; his ability to remember in great detail facts, figures, dates, and events; nor his ability to discuss current politics and business events with apparent ease. His language abilities seemed unaltered, and his physical coordination and functioning worked normally.

The tumor began to change him, however. Just as in the Phineas Gage story, Elliot's basic personality and social abilities were disrupted, and at the time Damasio began to see him, he was already under the supervised care of a sibling. Elliot had lost his first wife to divorce because of his condition, and his very brief second marriage was to a woman many thought an unlikely choice for the pre-tumor Elliot. He drifted about, unable to keep a schedule, wasting his resources, and losing all of his savings to ill-conceived business schemes.

Over a period of testing and reflection, Damasio and his colleague Daniel Tranel found that Elliot had lost his ability to emotionally connect with the world. Tranel presented images to Elliot of earthquakes, fires, floods, people battered in gory accidents—none of which could evoke an emotional response. Damasio began to form the idea that Elliot could know things but not feel them emotionally. Testing his idea, Damasio presented Elliot with a series of problem-solving situations that were comparable to the type of business situations Elliot had been very skilled at before developing the tumor. He easily and readily produced a variety of valid options for each of the situations presented. But after one test session, when finally asked which one of his many options he would pick, Elliot responded, "After all this, I still wouldn't know what to do!"[2]

The loss Elliot suffered shows how important the emotional system is to making sense and meaning in the world. All other functions seemed intact, yet the tumor knocked out his emotional system's ability to coordinate with the others. As a result, Elliot's life was as permanently altered as Gage's.

Symbolic System

Equally gifted at writing, Oliver Sacks has secured a following for his books on the quirky neurological afflictions that help us understand the brain and the human condition. Inventive book titles like *The Man Who Mistook His Wife for a Hat* and *An Anthropologist on Mars* have attracted and affected thousands who have enjoyed Sacks's poignant observations about the human condition.

One of his stories concerns the tender and fragile events of one of his patients, Rebecca. Clumsy, uncoordinated, possessed of a partially cleft palate, which caused whistling in her speech, and myopic to the point that she required Coke-bottle-thick eyeglasses, Rebecca was unfortunately regarded by others at the time (in the rather politically incorrect terms) as a klutz, moron, and retard. She was shy and withdrawn, as you might imagine, and when Sacks first saw her, when she was nineteen, it seemed she had the intellectual abilities of an eight-year-old.

What struck Sacks and makes his story of her condition so profound was Rebecca's ability to use metaphor, symbols, and stories in a wonderfully poetic manner. Especially when presented with calm, soothing surroundings, Rebecca was capable of stitching together the meaning of her life in a warm, lustrous tapestry that allowed her to understand and deal with even the gravest of events. Upon hearing that one of the most important people in her life, her grandmother, had passed away, Rebecca was understandably crushed. She dealt with the sense of this loss through her narrative abilities. When Sacks broke the news to her, he saw her reaction move from a state best described as frozen in grief to one of calm resignation as she cried over the death of her precious grandmother. What she said seems profound for a girl whose overall mental deficiencies were so marked. She first reacted to the news with statements such as "Why did she have to go?" and "I'm crying for her, not for me." After this initial reaction, her statements showed acceptance of the situation: "Grannie's all right. She's gone to her Long Home." This poetic idea was followed by "I'm so cold. It's not outside, it's winter inside. Cold as death. She was a part of me. Part of me died with her." After a while these allusions were followed by a deeper understanding and a prediction of the future when she said, "It is winter. I feel dead. But I know the spring will come again."[3]

Sacks saw in Rebecca the power of the narrative system, part of the overall systems of the brain that deal with stories, anecdotes, metaphor, mental pictures, similes, and other symbolic manipulations. Considering Rebecca, Sacks suggested that her case shows: "Very young children love and demand stories, and can understand complex matters presented as stories, when their powers of comprehending general concepts, paradigms, are almost non-existent. It is this narrative or symbolic power which gives a sense of the world—a concrete reality in the imaginative form of symbol and story—when abstract thought can provide nothing at all."[4]

After her grandmother's death, Rebecca rejected any further involvement in the workshops and other treatment processes that attempted to address her non-symbolic abilities. She told Sacks she needed meaning for her life and that the operational classes did nothing for her. As she stood before him, looking down at the carpet in his office she said, "I'm like a sort of living carpet. I need a pattern, a design, like you have on that carpet. I come apart, I unravel, unless there's a design."[5]

Sacks enrolled her in a theater group that allowed her to thrive. In fact, music and dance seemed to dissolve Rebecca's clumsiness and produce an athletic grace that was not apparent in everyday activities.

A Brain Update

Three case studies can't confirm a thesis, but they do serve to illustrate a wealth of stories that are similar in nature. These three stories are presented to demonstrate the distinction between the three systems: the factual, emotional, and symbolic. What they illustrate is that although each system can function independently, greater sense and meaning is constructed when all three systems cooperate. And most communication courses are restatements of various portions of these three systems even when they are taught using contemporary, inventive, and delightful language.

Rhetoric is a good thing to study in order to improve your communication abilities. Most rhetorical studies, however, revolve around the basic principles of logos (facts) and pathos (emotions). Symbolism, or what we refer to here as the symbolic system, refers to figures of speech, anecdotes, or stories that simply convey our logic and emotion. Symbolism is not generally seen as a separate cognitive agency by rhetoricians, but it is by cognitive scientists. Of course, ethos (the credibility of the communicator) is central to the basic rhetorical coursework. Whether you follow the classic works of Aristotle or the more contemporary versions of rhetoric or communication theory expounded by Kenneth Burke, Geoffrey Hartman, Kathleen Hall-Jamieson, Barbara Biesecker, Paul de Man, Jacques Derrida, Marshall McLuhan, or others, you can gain a deeper understanding of what rhetorical theories get right and what they miss by understanding how neurological systems that effect logic, emotion, and symbols work. Sense and meaning are created by the combination of these three systems.

Your Brain Doesn't Work Like a Computer

To start with, lose the brain-like-a-computer method of thinking. As Harvard Medical School's John H. Ratey points out, "The brain is nothing like the personal computers it has designed, for it does not process information and construct images by manipulating strings of digits such as ones and zeros. Instead, the brain is largely composed of maps, arrays of neurons that apparently represent entire objects of perception or cognition, or at least entire sensory or cognitive qualities of those objects, such as color, texture, credibility, or speed."[6] Scientists now know that the various lobes (frontal, occipital, temporal, parietal) are more densely interconnected than previously thought, and that there is no single center for vision, language, emotion, social behavior, consciousness, or memory. Older models that depict one chunk of the brain taking care of cognition, one taking care of emotion, one taking care of speech and the senses, and one taking care of automatic functions have been left to history's footnotes. Even the search for memory has been dramatically altered, as it is now understood that memories are not stored in a specific area (like a file on a computer) but are literally re-created by combining or recombining information from a vast network of systems. You could say your memory is only as good as your ability to re-create it.

Your Brain Seeks to Make Sense and Meaning All the Time

Second, we need to remember that all day, every day, our brains create sense and meaning out of a chaotic world. Neurologist Joseph LeDoux states, "One of the main jobs of consciousness is to keep our life tied together into a coherent story."[7] LeDoux suggests that human consciousness requires an explanation of what has happened, what is happening, and what will happen next filtered through an individual's sense of self and their perception of their physical environment. His observations are echoed by the insights garnered by neuroscientist V. S. Ramachandran, who suggests in his book *A Brief Tour of Human Consciousness: From Imposter Poodles to Purple Numbers* (another playful title from the world of brain science) that "the self" has five parts. These parts of the self do the following:

1. Create an unbroken sense of past, present, and future.

2. Provide a sense of unity—of being one person (assuming, of course, you do not have that rare "multiple personality" neurology).

3. Connect your mind with your body (which will become important in an illustration later on).

4. Establish a sense of agency or free will.

5. Provide self-awareness (that is, being able to know that you know).[8]

Making sense and meaning, then, requires being self-aware enough to be able to construct a coherent story about what's happened, what will happen, and what is going to happen to you. These ideas will become very important in our later discussion of how leaders gain alignment to organization vision and meaning.

Brain Movies

A third new idea is that since your brain doesn't work like a computer, a different comparison might help us make more sense of how it works. Damasio metaphorically describes brain functioning this way: "Most consciousness studies are actually centered on this issue of the making of the mind, the part of the consciousness puzzle that consists of having the brain make images that are synchronized and edited into what I have called the 'movie-in-the-brain.'"[9] While different from making a Hollywood, Bollywood, or Nollywood (Nigerian movie industry) movie (or an Apple iMovie, for that matter), the movie metaphor does help describe many of the ways in which the brain detects, creates, stores, retrieves, processes, and edits a variety of sensory inputs, memories, mental constructs, logical processes, and feelings. As Ratey puts it, "The brain assembles perceptions by the simultaneous interaction of whole concepts, whole images. Rather than using the predicative logic of a microchip, the brain is an analog processor, meaning, essentially, that it works by analogy and metaphor."[10]

As scientists have unraveled more and more of how the systems work, they have been on a mission to create new mental models that easily explain brain functioning, especially to non-specialists. Since computer technology leads to erroneous comparisons, the movie metaphor appears to be a new attempt at explaining complexity easily. "Movies are the closest external representation of the prevailing storytelling that goes on in our mind ... [W]hat goes on in the transition of shots achieved by editing, and what goes on in the narrative constructed by a particular juxtaposition of shots is comparable in some respects to what is going in the mind," Damasio explains.[11]

We decided to go with the scientists and use the movie metaphor as a way to help leaders understand that their communication works best when it creates a complete and compelling movie. And it seems that a complete movie uses information from the factual, emotional, and symbolic systems, regardless of what other information is processed. For example, for simplicity's sake, many neurologists present the logical and emotional systems as densely hardwired together. As Richard and Bernice Lazarus point out in their seminal book *Passion and Reason,* "[I]t is a careless—but common—usage to suggest that when we make bad decisions, they are based on emotion, but when we arrive at good decisions, they are based solely on reason."[12] The Lazaruses believe that there is no way to separate this entanglement. Logic and emotion combined help individuals make the best judgments.

There are more neurological pathways from the emotional system to the logical system than vice-versa. These pathways interact on every decision. Strong emotion can momentarily overpower our judgments and degrade our decision-making ability. Over-controlling, denying, or not effectively dealing with emotion can also degrade the quality of our decision making. Or, more important to the emotional or social intelligence theorists, lacking the ability to adequately or maturely process emotion can lead to less effective decision making. As LeDoux's rigorous research shows, "There is but one mechanism of consciousness and it can be occupied by mundane facts or highly charge emotions. Emotions easily bump mundane events out of awareness, but non-emotional events (like thoughts) do not so easily displace emotions from the mental spotlight—wishing that anxiety or depression would go away is usually not enough."[13]

Consider Phineas Gage's story. Critical portions of his frontal and prefrontal logic systems were destroyed by the accident, leaving the emotional system chronically out of control. His social abilities were eroded, his long-term planning ability was apparently eradicated, and his emotional demeanor and moods turned unpredictable and intense. The emotional system hijacked his life, because it couldn't interact with his logical system. As Ratey explains, "The frontal cortex is the part of the brain that neatly organizes the bits and pieces into a temporal, logical, and 'meaningful' story. However, it must be set in motion by the amygdala, which provides an emotional tag to a memory, a 'meaning' that helps cement the pieces."[14] Gage, once a well-liked, thoughtful engineer with a promising career, lost his ability to create and maintain a movie for his life, because his emotions had no facts or logic to hang on to.

Elliot's story is the reverse. This man lost critical emotional functions through disease, and even though his logical and symbolic systems remained intact, he lost his ability to decide. His logical system could not interact with his emotional system, and he remains chronically indecisive, even over trivial matters.

Another series of interesting studies concern gamblers who have the ability to consistently win at blackjack at such high levels that they are regularly banned from casinos. Studying the logical-emotional connection for these individuals indicates that they seem to have high pattern recognition and other cognitive skills, but low emotional skills. They can win at the game of blackjack, but generally are lost in the game of life.

It is not just the logical and emotional channels that interact, however. In order for a movie to be made, the symbolic channel must be added. This channel is complex. In the opening chapter we grabbed cupfuls of research from the communication tsunami. Switching metaphors now, we want to provide a collage of quotes about the symbolic channel.

"The ability to perceive objects and events, external to the organism or internal to it, requires images. Examples of the images related to the exterior include visual, auditory, tactile, olfactory, and gustatory images. Pain and nausea are examples of images of the interior. The execution of both automatic and deliberated responses requires images. The anticipation and planning of future responses also requires images."[15]

"Different kinds of memory, like different kinds of emotions and different kinds of sensations, come out of different brain systems."[16]

"Language is, indeed, the ultimate symbolic mental function, and it is virtually impossible to conceive of thought as we know it in its absence."[17]

"You don't have a choice as to whether to think metaphorically. Because metaphorical maps are part of our brains, we will think and speak metaphorically whether we want to or not."[18]

"A key—perhaps the key—to leadership is the effective communication of a story."[19]

"Even the most recondite scientific reasoning is an assembly of down-home mental metaphors."[20]

"Telling stories ... is probably a brain obsession and probably begins relatively early both in terms of evolution and in terms of the complexity. Telling stories precedes language, since it is, in fact, a condition for language, and it is based not just in the cerebral cortex but elsewhere in the brain and in the right hemisphere as well as the left."[21]

"To this day, nouns are found in the temporal lobe, verbs in the frontal lobe across the Sylvian fissure. It was their coming together that transformed a protolanguage of symbols and signs into a true grammatical language."[22]

Rebecca's story is a poignant example of how metaphor and other symbolism is a separately functioning mental process that profoundly interacts with the logical and emotional systems, even when the functioning of these systems is compromised.

In summary, a complex series of interactions between the logical, emotional, and symbolic channels combine to create the rapidly changing movie in our minds. We edit the images in a flash, recombine details as new information arrives or is created, and store information so that when we reimagine it (reimage it), we can relate it well. When we found high-quality communication occurring with leaders, it was always accompanied by information flowing from all three channels. And now we know why. It takes all three channels to form the most compelling image, to complete a movie, to make sense and meaning. Good communicators know how to provide information so that constituents can create a total movie.

Filling In the Blanks

Because all three channels are required to make a movie, if a leader doesn't convey information on all three channels, constituents must fill in the blanks from their own, internal sources. Steven Pinker points out, "The mind reflexively interprets other people's words and gestures by doing whatever it takes to make them sensible and true. If the words are sketchy or incongruous, the mind charitably fills in missing premises or shifts to a new frame of reference in which they make sense."[23]

This is a dangerous condition. Getting your meaning and message through is hard enough without constituents' minds filling in the blanks. And unfortunately, many of us work under the premise that our memories are infallible, operating like permanently recorded DVDs or computer memory. That's not the case. Elizabeth Loftus, a noted psychologist and expert on eyewitness testimony, says the following in her article about how people make stuff up if they have to create a memory: "People tend to think of memory ... that we have all these videotapes of events stored somewhere in the brain if only we can find them."[24] She explains that memories are re-created each time we remember, and that while some memories can be re-created with high fidelity, the reality is that they also change. Put in neurological terms, Ratey explains, "The formation and recall of each memory are influenced by mood, surroundings, and gestalt at the time the memory is formed or retrieved. Each one arises from a vast network of interconnected pieces. The pieces are units of language, emotions, beliefs, and actions, and here, right away, comes the first surprising conclusion: because our daily experiences constantly alter these connections, a memory is a tiny bit different each time we remember it."[25]

Memory is stimulated constantly through internal and external events. "A memory is only made when it is called upon. We cannot separate the act of retrieving and the memory itself. Indeed, bits and pieces of a single memory are stored in different networks of neurons all around the brain."[26] But we don't remember things until we need to. When a leader communicates, he or she is striving to have constituents recall a common memory, whether that memory involves a policy, strategy, or organizational mission or vision. These conditions lead us to two big ideas about communicating movies:

1. If the leader doesn't provide information on all three channels, constituents will. It is the only way they can complete their understanding—make a mental movie.

2. Repetition of a key message, or central movie (the focus of our next chapter), is crucial to keeping the organization aligned and regulating the natural process that leads individual and organizational movies over time to change—sometimes into totally different movies from what the leader is trying to communicate.

Meaningful Movies

We are all actors in the miniseries of our lives, and work is often a dominant story line to most individuals' lives. Leaders create an organizational movie of the future and ask constituents to buy in—that's vision. Constituents want a role in a movie that makes sense and meaning to them—that's engagement. Constituents' minds constantly process leaders' descriptions of the future, calls to action, business analyses, or commentaries on hundreds of day-to-day dynamics. As they listen and edit these messages, they re-create (update) or fill in the blanks (originate) a movie that answers questions like:

- How will my job change?
- Can I get this done in addition to all the work I already have to do?
- Does this mean more layoffs?
- How does this new information change what is already going on?
- What opportunities does this provide me?
- How will all of this affect my income?
- Am I capable of what will be required of me?
- What if I fail?
- What if we fail?
- How will we succeed?
- Where are going?

When the questions are answered and constituents see a role, perhaps a starring role, in this compelling movie, they sign on. That's alignment, the perennially illusive competence, everyone making the same movie. Screenwriting lecturer Robert McKee was interviewed about how to convey powerful business communication. He explained an important concept when he said,

> You [meaning the CEO] say, "Here is our company's biggest challenge, and here is what we need to do to prosper." And you build your case by giving statistics and facts and quotes from authorities. But there are two problems with rhetoric. First, the people you're talking to have their own set of authorities, statistics, and experiences. While you're trying to persuade them, they are arguing with you in their heads. Second, if you do succeed in persuading them, you've done so only on an intellectu-

al basis. That's not good enough, because people are not inspired to act by reason alone.[27]

Communication flows on three channels: factual, emotional, and symbolic. Any communication that does not adequately attend to one of these channels leaves the leader open to one of the four fatal assumptions of communication. Constituents use their own logic and experience, beliefs and biases, to construct sense and meaning. They choose how they view the message and what they will do about it. It is fundamentally important to understand that the only way for the brain to make a movie—that is, to create sense and meaning—is to combine facts, emotions, and symbols.

If the facts, emotions, and symbols are shared with others, then the likelihood is greater that the group will participate in a shared movie. Yet within this shared movie, people want to see themselves in the movie. We all want the chance to add a line, a scene, or a plot.

Using these three channels well is like a painter using the three primary colors well, or like a pianist using basic chords well. Three primary colors, and their combination, create images ranging from refrigerator art to Picassos. Eleven octaves, and their combination, create piano music ranging from chopsticks to Rachmaninoff's Piano Concerto no. 3, the famous piece that drove Geoffrey Rush's character nearly insane in his Oscar-winning performance in the movie *Shine.* Three channels of communication create meaning ranging from "See Spot Run," to memorable lines like the following from Shakespeare's *MacBeth:*

> Tomorrow, and tomorrow, and tomorrow,
> Creeps in this petty pace from day to day,
> To the last syllable of recorded time;
> And all our yesterdays have lighted fools
> The way to dusty death. Out, out, brief candle!
> Life's but a walking shadow, a poor player,
> That struts and frets his hour upon the stage,

And then is heard no more. It is a tale
Told by an idiot, full of sound and fury,
Signifying nothing.[28]

Using the channels well helps constituents imagine a stirring, powerful movie, one that allows them to create personal roles that move the plot along. Most people are looking for a calling, not just a job. We want to defy MacBeth's declaration that life is a meaningless series of events that pass time until oblivion arrives. Alignment occurs not just because the three channels were used to invite others to your organization's calling, its mission, or its purpose, but because they were used well, moving constituents to willingly act in a movie worthy of their blood, sweat, and tears.

3

THE CENTRAL MOVIE

Execution made a sparkling return appearance, as best actor on the leadership stage, right after the business downturn in the early part of this millennium's first decade. Like many leadership topics that recycle their way through our attention, it has had a powerful scene or two and has sounded with fury, but will soon exit, stage left, right, or trapdoor. Some believe it is the current reincarnation of that beloved business uncle known as total quality management. Execution as a management topic and business imperative deserves a great deal of credit, for when it acts well, audiences are delighted. But execution alone cannot answer the question "why?"

We are bothered by questions of why. Why do I exist? Why do people do the things they do? Why do I work at this job? Why do I have these relationships? Why is my society not living up to its ideals? As noted in the previous chapter, our minds incessantly attempt to answer the "why?" questions, because the answers help us establish context, understanding, or control. And our brains will not stop searching until these issues of greater attention and scope, these issues of purpose, have at least an adequate, and hopefully profound, answer.

Take a look at the following quotes and leaders. For fun, see if you can match the quote to the leader.

"We have a secret weapon—it is called Nationalism."

"It is a kingly act to assist the fallen."

"Man is not free unless government is limited."

"You can chain me, you can torture me, you can even destroy this body, but you will never imprison my mind."

"You may have to fight a battle more than once to win it."

"The art of leadership is saying no, not saying yes. It is very easy to say yes."

"Weapons are an important factor in war, but not the decisive factor; it is people, not things, that are decisive."

"Global poverty is a powder keg that could be ignited by our indifference."

"Injustice anywhere is a threat to justice everywhere."

"We don't appreciate what we have until it's gone. Freedom is like that. It's like air. When you have it, you don't notice it."

"If a free society cannot help the many who are poor, it cannot save the few who are rich."

"Better to die standing than to live on your knees."

"Education is the most powerful weapon which you can use to change the world."

"Fear is a habit, and I am not afraid."

"Success is the ability to go from one failure to another with no loss of enthusiasm."

Margaret Thatcher

Boris Yeltsin

Mother Teresa

John F. Kennedy

Bill Clinton

Winston Churchill

Mao Zedong

Mahatma Gandhi

Ho Chi Minh

Martin Luther King Jr.

Ernesto "Che" Guevara

Aung San Suu Kyi

Tony Blair

Nelson Mandela

Ronald Reagan

See answers to quiz on page 53 at end of chapter.

Quotes such are these are memorable "sound bites" attached to central movies that these particular leaders were attempting to put voice to in an effort to answer the "why" question. Central movies are the main context, the big idea, and the expression of where we are going. They answer why this destination is important, how we are going to get there, and how this makes sense with regard to our ideals. Central movies are how individual leaders, during short periods of history, put voice to enduring organizational ideologies that generally evolve slowly. The following diagram provides a way of viewing this idea.

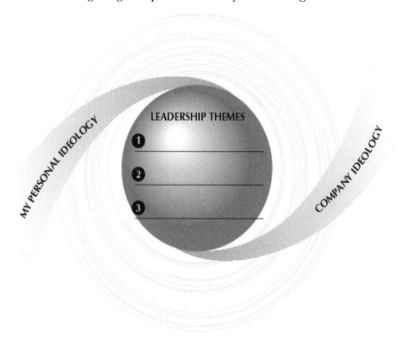

A leader gives voice to an organization's ideology, its raison d'être, its central purpose and mission. We are more apt to follow leaders who are able to communicate that ideology most powerfully. Yet all leaders put voice to the collective group through their own personal ideology. In the best cases the leader amplifies the organization's ideology in a manner that clarifies, uplifts, confirms, or energizes individuals' belief in and willingness to work toward this ideology. An audience, whether it's your small project team or the entire organization, detects and distinguishes the differences between the individual leader and the organization he or she represents. An audience also detects the unity or congruence between a leader and the organization, as leaders often become the embodiment of the organization's voice. The best communicators confer a personal inflection to the organization's central movie, this main purpose or ideology. The best leaders enhance such communication by embodying this central movie through their actions. When an authentic and practiced voice is catalyzed with superior social intelligence, the result is a compelling leader—a leader whose voice will be heard.

Themes: Building Blocks for a Central Movie

Sidney Lumet received a Lifetime Achievement Oscar in 2005. He was an actor before he was a director, and while many of the movies he directed have achieved acclaim, some have been critical and financial duds. Many commercial and governmental leaders have enjoyed similar careers. Although the creation of a Lumet-type movie is similar to the central movie of an organization, the limits of this comparison have been detailed in chapter 2. One of the places where the comparison is worthy of another look is in themes.

Themes are the building blocks for your central movie. The idea of a commercial leader's central movie can often be compared to, but not necessarily limited to, any one of these other business terms: vision, strategic intent, mission, brand promise, differentiation strategy, organizational values, or brand image. Each of these terms refers to a high-level abstraction about the purpose or intent that holds the organization together. An organizational ideology is comprised of all of these things. Ideology is experienced by what we say and what we do. At high levels of abstraction, an organizational ideology includes the collective statements and actions comprised of what we stand for (brand promise, brand image, intent), how we act (values), long-term goals (vision, strategy), and how we will go about our work (operating methods, differentiation strategy).

An individual's ideology, however, is comprised of different elements. Individual ideology derives from the combination of personality, style, lifetime experiences, inherited and developed beliefs and values, and world views shaped by reflection and experience. Every leader, consciously or not, amplifies or constrains, illuminates or obscures, and inspires or fatigues the central movie they lead through their personal voice and action. Lumet's best movies stayed true to their central theme, or high-level abstractions. Commercial leaders' best organizational successes occur when they do the same.

Today's commercial world is fast paced and over-stimulated. It can be quite daunting to strain and sift understanding from the constant barrage of messages we receive from an increasing number of sources. Central movies help us sort the essential from the nonessential, the timely from the timeless, and the operational from the semantic. Themes are the individual leaders' way of saying in their own voice what the organization's central movie means during their tenure. They are the personal expressions of high-abstraction ideas that help any individual leader—in their voice, in their style, in their way—put voice to the meaning of the organizational ideology, the organization's central movie.

An example will help illustrate the idea. Imagine if you will that you want to run for president of the United States. (As this book is being written in 2008, you may as well imagine this, since so many have already started campaigning.) In order to run for this office, any candidate must put voice to the United States' central ideology or central movie. To keep this illustration straightforward and as politically neutral as possible, let's take a look at just four primary components of this country's ideology.

Universal Principles : freedom, democracy, constitutional government, equality

Long-term Goals : education, security, "life, liberty, pursuit of happiness"

Operating Methods: free markets, capitalism, due process, federal and state governments

Values: Bill of Rights, Constitution, separation of
                               church and state

Consider any of the statements at the beginning of this chapter by
any of the American leaders who put voice to these ideological aspirations (Attention! The following discussion provides hints to the
quote-matching quiz.) Kennedy and Clinton put voice to long-term
goals by drawing attention to the poor. King put voice to universal
principles with his statements and stands against injustice. Reagan
put voice to operating methods by his concerns about the limits of
government process. In similar light, you could look at Ho Chi
Minh's constant themes of nationalism and freedom during his long
leadership, or Thatcher's theme of perseverance in order to change, or
Mandela's theme of education as a foundation to nation building.

To continue the illustration, let's look a little closer at a former U.S.
president, Ronald Reagan. To see how he developed the consistent
themes of his eight years in office, we must consider a sketch of his
personal ideology.

Personality: gregarious, self-effacing

Experiences: small-town childhood, movie actor, World
                               War II service, Screen Actor's Guild president
                               during the McCarthy era, involved in local
                               and state politics, California governor for two
                               terms, two lost bids for presidential nomina-
                               tion, two terms as U.S. president

Values/Beliefs: determined self-effort, rugged individualism,
                               optimistic

World views: government should be limited, stand up to
                               dangers to democracy

Reagan was a self-starter, born and raised in modest circumstances
in a small town. His natural optimism seemed to be enhanced by that
of his mother, and he developed regard for hard work, simplifying
complex issues, and taking on big challenges. Reagan's personal ideology, over the course of his life, led him to develop five themes that

underscored his interpretation of American ideology. These themes can be stated as:

- American's greatness
- rugged individualism
- limited government
- evil empire
- hope for tomorrow

Reagan applied these themes as his way of explaining the American central movie during his tenure.

Others have used themes in a similar manner. For instance, Nelson Mandela's legendary resistance to a government he could not support over twenty-seven years of imprisonment has led to his development of forgiveness, unity, education, and determination themes. Boris Yeltsin's democratic reforms, often cast in hard-hitting statements and actions termed "shock therapy," used actions almost as much as words to declare his themes for a democratic, economic reformation of his country, defying what he felt was a corrupt Moscow machine. One obituary stated, "Mr. Yeltsin stood for three fundamental principles. He believed in freedom of speech, including freedom of the press, no matter what. He wanted Russia to be friends with the west. And he despised the Communist party."[2] History likely will cast him as a flawed hero, but the themes of his central movie, a movie of tremendous change for an entire society, were clear. His posture astride a tank, defying a coup, is a hard-to-forget moment of symbolic communication. And Burma's Aung San Suu Kyi, recipient of the 1991 Nobel Peace Prize and 1992 Jawaharlal Nehru peace prize, has remained steadfast to her refrain that fear, not power, is the ultimate corruptor. Time will determine whether or not the central movie of her National League for Democracy will win out.

Thematic Evolution

Any organization's central movie will change over time. Some organizations, such as stable government systems, will see adaptations to their ideology change more slowly over time than most commercial enterprises. Revolutions do occur, which usher in rapid, sometimes huge, changes to the ideology. When this changes, the movie changes. Abrupt changes require leaders to not only recast the movie but to also find multiple ways of repeating it in order for its dimension and scope to conform to and explain the changes in reality.

Examples of these changes are chronicled in the case studies you'll find in chapter 4. These studies show how leaders in two different organizations, LensCrafters and TNT, used all three channels to gain support for changes in corporate ideologies. In LensCrafters' case, the evolution occurred along the lines of a start-up organization that grew rapidly and successfully and had to evolve an initial movie to match its own organizational scope and reach. In the TNT case, the change was more abrupt and represents how an organization with a hugely successful ideology and movie had to adapt to rapid industry changes.

Regardless of the pace of change, leaders can easily and naturally become absorbed with just the tasks of staying on top of operational progress and fixing problems. Lumet once wrote, "My job is to care about and be responsible for every frame of every movie I make."[3] Many commercial leaders feel the same way about their businesses. Whether they're facing big or small problems, they roll up their sleeves and work. This often leaves little time for communication—helping make sense of all the action, change, and distraction. Taking care of each frame, without confirming again and again what the movie is all about, can lead to disengagement. People will work on today's frame or scene, but without the passion of being part of a really important movie.

Howard Gardner's book *Changing Minds* explores his thesis that for a person to change his or her own mind, or to effect a change of mind in others, seven factors (or levers, as he sometimes terms them) may be involved that will facilitate the change or help maintain the change once it is made. His seven levers are reason, research, resonance, representational redescriptions, resources and rewards, real-world events, and resistances.[4] Gardner's thesis sheds light on what is required of leaders who are attending to the evolution of thematic changes in their central movie while at the same time having to attend to the details of each and every frame. This is especially true when the theme has been tarnished and leadership is suspect. Each of his seven levers can be practically used to help clarify and underscore thematic changes. The following example will illustrate how three of these levers—reason, resonance, and real-world events were used for a short time to help many people engage with the enduring organizational themes of a well-known organization.

Olympic Fire

Pierre de Frédy, Baron de Coubertin, was the inspirer and organizer of the revival of the international Olympic Games, the first modern games being held in Athens, Greece, in 1896. An energetic man immersed in the sports of boxing, fencing, rowing, and horse riding, he did not accept his parents' wishes of pursuing a military or political career, but decided to renew France's interest in education. The real-world event that is most often cited as having influenced his view on education is France's loss in the Franco-Prussian War of 1870. This defeat occurred when Coubertin was seven years old, and as he reflected on it later, he determined the loss did not result from a lack of military tactics as much as underdeveloped individual vigor. And he believed vigor could be developed through sports. During his late twenties Coubertin reviewed the educational systems of Germany, Britain, France, and the United States and decided that a change of mind about physical education would renew the vigor with which France would approach learning and education.

Thinking big, Coubertin didn't simply decide to start a school with a robust sports agenda or try to convince the French school system to change its mind about curriculum. He decided to renew France's interest, along with that of the rest of the world, by reestablishing the Olympic Games. After a couple of false starts and a difficult time in arousing interest, he finally founded the International Olympic Committee in 1894. Symbolically, the surrounding ceremonial events were held at the University of Sorbonne in Paris, and Demetrius Vikelus of Greece was selected to become the organization's first president.

Coubertin attended to resonance by attaching his ideas of Olympic revival to thematic debates of the times. During this middle period of the Industrial Revolution, the two colossal social pressures of free trade and peace were pushing on Europe like tectonic plates. These two themes are still alive in different ways today, despite the unfortunate episodic conflicts that have accompanied the change since 1870. At a meeting of the Union des Sports Athlétiques in Paris on November 25, 1892, Coubertin stated:

> Let us export our oarsmen, our runners, our fencers into other lands. That is the true Free Trade of the future; and the day it is introduced into Europe the cause of Peace will have received a new and strong ally. It inspires me to touch upon another step I now propose and in it I shall ask that the help you have given me hitherto you will extend again, so that together we may attempt to realise, upon a basis suitable to the conditions of our modern life, the splendid and beneficent task of reviving the Olympic Games.[5]

These same thoughts are echoed in the modern Olympic Movement, as evidenced on the International Olympic Committee Web site, dedicated to continuing Coubertin's ideals about the Olympics. These ideals (part of the overall Olympic ideology) are "to contribute to building a peaceful and better world by educating youth through sport practised without discrimination of any kind and in the Olympic spirit, which requires mutual understanding with a spirit of friendship, solidarity and fair play."[6]

Vying for the honor of being the host city for the Olympic Games is fraught with difficulties, often shrouded with skepticism concerning scruples, and always politically charged. Once a city has been selected, however, despite the bumpy selection process, the games must go on. Each city, hosting each new installment of the Olympic Games, whether summer or winter, wants to add a distinct chapter to the Olympic story. Here's part of what happened at the 2002 Winter Games in Salt Lake City.

The Fire Within

Just past midnight on February 5, 2002, Bob Chambers stood waist-deep in snow, six thousand feet up the side of Twin Peaks Mountain. The wind chilled the temperature to zero. Bob held a seven-foot pole in one hand and a cell phone in the other. His L. L. Bean Two-Layer Duofold underwear kept his body warm, but passion warmed his heart. He was living a day in the history of Pierre Coubertin's Olympic vision. Working toward this particular moment, Chambers hadn't thought about the scandal or bribery that had plagued the beginning of the Salt Lake games. He hadn't thought much about the money his company would make. "This," he said, "was the highlight of my career."[7]

From the steps of Utah's capitol building, 1952 giant slalom gold medalist and Utah resident Stein Ericksen pointed the Olympic torch toward Twin Peaks and Bob flipped the switch. In an instant, the compact fluorescent light bulbs sitting atop 1,850 poles illuminated five giant interlocking rings stretching more than three football fields across the mountain. At the same time, fireworks exploded and the crowd cheered. Over the next seventeen days, more than three billion people would see the "floating rings," which were large enough to be seen from outer space.

Scott Givens served as managing director for the creative group of the Salt Lake Organizing Committee (SLOC). He had been charged with disseminating the theme "Light the Fire Within," first developed by creative ad man Gordon Bowen. In March 2000 the organizing committee's president, Mitt Romney, endorsed the theme and it was announced to the world. It could have been another Olympics, another theme. But as Romney said at the time, "We were able to align the interest of the various parties, because we all share, as a human family, some pretty common values."[8] Romney, Givens, Fraser Bullock, and other leaders were committed to making the theme of "the fire within" more than another catch phrase; they envisioned it as being an expression of the common desire to make a difference.

Givens set the design criteria that helped the creative group of people who became the nucleus of spreading the theme to vendors and volunteers. He prepared a five-page outline that defined who they were and who they weren't. "I wrote hard and fast rules," he said, using the theme's intensity and the rules to unite sponsors, vendors, and volunteers even as they each added their own special touch. For Givens's artists and writers, the reasons behind the theme's rules resonated and "allowed us to be more creative, because we knew who we were."

But Givens didn't write the rules in a vacuum. "Mitt Romney and I had long conversations," he said. "We could get an A in the opening ceremonies, an A in the medal presentations, and an A at the venues, but we needed all the A's to be aligned in order to become valedictorians." The SLOC realized that they had the chance to put voice to the enduring one-hundred-year-old ideology of the modern Olympics despite the difficult start, and their theme lit the way. They started with a Coca-Cola-sponsored torch relay. More than 100,000 aspiring torch bearers wrote stories explaining why they wanted to carry the metal-and-glass torch across the country, a torch lit with a flame inside. The relay event organizers selected 11,500 runners from these entries.

The theme spread via what Howard Gardner would term "representational redescriptions." This is a technical-sounding term that simply means if any idea is represented in a number of different ways, it will be easier to adopt by a broader base of individuals. A vendor at the Salt Lake City games suggested the "Children of Light" idea for the opening ceremony. Carrying small lanterns, children escorted every participant to the stand. From cool blues to hot oranges, the colors of the banners and signs around the venues communicated the theme. The International Olympic Committee, for the first time, allowed the theme of the games to be etched into each and every Olympic medal awarded. Everyone was beginning to add their own personal voice and touch to the event. This is perhaps the most visible and inspiring evidence of alignment to the central movie.

"Alignment was not forced," Givens said. It's impractical and likely impossible to force alignment upon thousands of employees, thousands of volunteers, and hundreds of vendors for a never-to-be-repeated seventeen-day event. Inspiring alignment through consistent communication of thought and deed can work. Once "the fire within" caught on, these disparate constituencies knew what to do. From small business vendors like Bob Chambers's It's Alive Company to large sponsors like Coca-Cola, the clarity of the theme helped.

Haven Riviere was responsible for Coca-Cola's multimillion-dollar sponsorship. "The theme was consistent all the way through. That was extremely important to us," he said. "If they had changed, people would not have seen the connection between what they were doing and what we were doing. The powerful thing that Salt Lake did was to recognize that the athletes, viewers, fans, and marketing sponsors all needed to see the same thing."[9]

It paid off. The Olympics' Winter Games never outperform the Summer Games, yet the Salt Lake Winter Games brought in more sponsorship than the Atlanta Summer Games. Here are some of the results of the Salt Lake Olympic Games:

- Produced 35,000 job years of employment and a total income of $1.5 billion.[10]
- Worldwide coverage was 50 percent greater than the 1998 Nagano games and 170 percent greater than Lillehammer.[11]
- 250,000 visitors spent an estimated $350 million over the course of the games.[12]
- The Salt Lake games repaid Utah $59 million in diverted sales tax revenue.[13]
- Salt Lake City realized a total economic impact of $4.8 billion.[14]

Coubertin had a difficult time arousing interest for the Olympics. And despite the modern-day difficulty of managing a challenging multinational political landscape that the business of the Olympics can be, perhaps it is good to remember that the fire within can still create a movie that allows people to come together in a great tradition and engage in some of the best work of their lives. Sports writer Bill Pennington of the *New York Times* wrote, "Ultimately, the Salt Lake games conferred upon the Olympic movement a modern blueprint for how to run a Winter Games that are cozy, attractive to a younger audience, and with significance and sizzle."[15]

Developing Your Themes

The following suggestions may help you put voice to the central movie of your organization. Don't be fooled by the simplicity of the ideas; if you actually try these suggestions, be prepared for some hard, but ultimately helpful, work.

Organizational Background

Research the history of your organization. Explore the foundations, find out about the founders or other significant leaders who grappled with the organization over time. If you are part of a start-up, take some time to speak with the founders about what really got them going. Try to dig beneath the surface of the company Web site's historical blurbs and find the stories of origin, stories of difficulties, and stories of success. Speak with people who have been around for a long time, and get them to reminisce about the good old days (and bad old days, if there are any). Talk with customers, partners, or suppliers. Find out what they think about the organization. Ask them what has changed over time.

Deep Personal Drive

Take time out to revisit who you are at heart. Dust off that Myers-Briggs profile, that 360-degree feedback, or take a values profile or personality assessment. If you are not a big believer in such approaches, then conduct your own fact-finding research on yourself. Find methods that will allow family, friends, work colleagues, teachers, coaches, clergy, or others to provide you with their viewpoints on the kind of person they believe you are. Compare their views with an exploration of what you really believe about yourself. If you have found an organization that you love working with and are generally happy in your job, figure out why that is true for you.

If you think the organization you are working in is messed up beyond belief, write down all the solutions you think would straighten things out. Then review your list of solutions. What do these solutions suggest to you about how you think about things, what values you feel are important, what processes you find work the best, or what world views you might hold?

Explain Your Work to a Stranger

After you have completed some background research and taken a deep dive into your personal views, put all of that information together. Using your own language, your own perspective, develop a three- to four-minute explanation of what you do and what your organization stands for. Find someone you don't know, and figure out a way to get that person to listen to your explanation. Your goal is to see if what you tell this stranger is clear and understandable and perhaps even compelling. After you have tried it out on a couple of strangers, run it by your group and see what happens.

Quiz Answers from Quiz on Page 40

Margaret Thatcher—"You may have to fight a battle more than once to win it."

Boris Yeltsin—"We don't appreciate what we have until it's gone. Freedom is like that. It's like air. When you have it, you don't notice it."

Mother Teresa—"It is a kingly act to assist the fallen."

John F. Kennedy—"If a free society cannot help the many who are poor, it cannot save the few who are rich."

Bill Clinton—"Global poverty is a powder keg that could be ignited by our indifference."

Winston Churchill—"Success is the ability to go from one failure to another with no loss of enthusiasm."

Mao Zedong—"Weapons are an important factor in war, but not the decisive factor; it is people, not things, that are decisive."

Mahatma Gandhi—"You can chain me, you can torture me, you can even destroy this body, but you will never imprison my mind."

Ho Chi Minh—"We have a secret weapon – it is called Nationalism."

Martin Luther King, Jr.—"Injustice anywhere is a threat to justice everywhere."

Ernesto "Che" Guevara—"Better to die standing, than to live on your knees."

Aung San Suu Kyi—"Fear is a habit, and I am not afraid."

Tony Blair—"The art of leadership is saying no, not saying yes. It is very easy to say yes."

Nelson Mandela—"Education is the most powerful weapon which you can use to change the world."

Ronald Reagan—"Man is not free unless government is limited."

4

TNT AND LENSCRAFTERS

How TNT Found Drama

TNT is one of cable television's great success stories. Created and launched by Ted Turner in 1988, its audience grew from 17 million to more than 50 million in less than two years. In the early days, the Atlanta-based TNT was known for its Westerns and classic movies, which the network leveraged from the MGM film library that Turner had purchased.[1]

As the network grew, it added World Championship Wrestling, NFL, NBA, and the Winter Olympics. Production of original movies became a centerpiece of its programming. Historical dramas such as Gettysburg, Andersonville, and George Wallace earned big ratings and were praised by critics. Throughout the 1990s, TNT consistently delivered some of cable's highest ratings. In 1996 TNT ranked number one in prime time, thanks to the power of the NFL, NBA, and WCW, and scored four of the top ten highest-rated movies on basic cable. Advertised as the "best movie studio on television," the network defined itself internally with its positioning statement: "TNT is for upscale adult couples and families looking for quality-driven television. TNT is the premiere basic cable network offering a variety of blue-chip sports and entertainment programs."

TNT continued to dominate through its ten-year anniversary in 1998. NASCAR, PGA, and Wimbledon were acquired. Tiger Woods,

Venus Williams, John Stockton, and others could be seen on the network. TNT's original movies earned big numbers, rave reviews, and attracted marquee Hollywood stars. In 1999 TNT again captured four of the top five highest-rated original movies on basic cable. In 2000 TNT's *Nuremberg* and *Running Mates* tied as the highest-rated original movies. By this time TNT was in more than 80 million homes, which at the time was 97 percent of American homes with cable or satellite television. The network reaped substantial profits from both cable subscriptions and advertising.

In 1999 Bradley J. Siegel, who was serving as president of the Turner Broadcasting System (TBS) brands TNT (Turner Network Television) and TCM (Turner Classic Movies), was promoted to president of general entertainment networks. This meant he now had to manage the TNT, TCM, TBS Superstation, and Turner South businesses. TNT was the number one cable network, and Siegel knew he had been given a terrific opportunity. He was concerned, however, about the rapid changes occurring in the industry. The late 1990s was the bend in the proverbial hockey stick in terms of the number of new entrants that were bursting cable's bandwidth. Stories about the new millennium's promise to provide five hundred or more information channels abounded. Brands such as FOX, A&E, Lifetime, and the powerful HBO were creating strong brand identities with more narrow and focused offerings than the all-variety broadcast networks, which TNT had modeled itself after.

Somewhat defying tradition, Siegel hired Steve Koonin from Coca-Cola as COO. Siegel had been friends with Koonin for a few years and had admired his work at Coca-Cola. He wanted someone who understood branding and who was from outside the industry, counting on this perspective as a valuable asset to reimagine the company. As soon as he arrived at his job, Koonin said, "We are in a category of general entertainment and, boy, when you're general, your nothing."

Koonin got to work quickly to start gathering factual evidence about what TNT was up against. He is known for his robust humor and love of alliteration. He started touting his three P's for redirection: "We need to POSITION the network, PROGRAM to the positioning, and then PROMOTE the programming and positioning."

What Viewers Thought of TNT

TNT traditionally had broadcast everything from Hulk Hogan smashing bodies to Juliette Binoche falling in love in *The English Patient.* By design they wanted to appeal to a wide audience and offer programming that connected with all audience segments. "Focus was the f-word," said Scot Safon, TNT's senior vice president of marketing. "It meant you'd be deliberately limiting your appeal."

Ratings were strong when Koonin arrived, but as his fact finders found, viewers didn't know what to expect from TNT. Viewers identified with the brands of Lifetime (women), ESPN (sports), MTV (music), and other TNT competitors. In one series of focus group interviews, TNT staff asked customers to draw a picture of what they thought TNT was all about. They simply asked, "What does TNT stand for?"

These representative scribbles drawn by adult viewers confirmed the executives' worst fears: TNT stood for everything instead of something. As Koonin put it, "We were known for our parts, while other networks were known for the sum of their parts. It was time to position or perish."

To add a strong dose of drama to TNT's situation, Koonin and his team had to turn a big billion dollar ship in the midst of a "Perfect Storm." TNT was launching its first brand initiative during the worst media market in a lifetime, while TNT and Turner Broadcasting were being merged along with the rest of Time Warner into AOL. Ad sales were down, budgets were being cut, and layoffs were required. For a few months in early 2001, nervous questions swirled through the hallways at 1050 Techwood Street: "Has your project been killed?"

"Did you hear so-and-so was let go?" "Are we moving our offices to New York?" And to top things off, the entire senior-level executive team at Turner Broadcasting was shuffled right in the middle of the brand initiative.

So to chart this course Koonin assembled a fantastic team of people around him. They were, to name a few, Scot Safon in marketing, Jennifer Dorian on branding, Karen Cassell managing public relations, Jon Marks conducting the research, Michael Borza and Ron Korb handing the on-air creative, and Ken Schwab in programming.

The TNT team did their research, analyzed the competition, and listened to their customers and associates. They formulated hypothetical brand positions reflecting TNT's heritage. They rigorously studied network attributes, perceptual maps, and viewer segmentation studies. During the research phase of the branding initiative, Koonin and his team took the unusual and welcome step of involving the entire staff, something rarely if ever done in the network world. "We shared research with everyone," he said, "but we made it easy to understand."

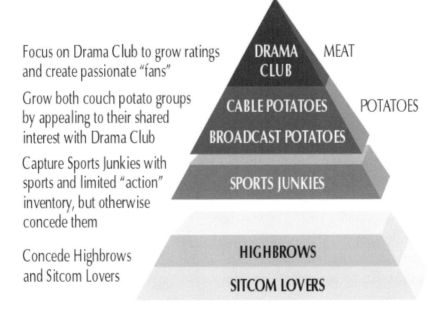

The data began to reveal a pattern that could be represented in a "food pyramid" type of graphic. Fundamentally, the team began to see that what they referred to as the Drama Club, the pyramid's pinnacle, consisted of only 20 percent of the market. However, these viewers were affluent, and when viewing their twenty-four hours a week of programming they wanted material that was emotionally engaging and/or made them think.

Since the research was being shared, it was clear for everyone to see that TNT needed to position itself as "100 percent dramatic entertainment that makes you think and feel." The Drama Club represented both TNT's strongest audience and its best prospects for growth.

There is always a vulnerable moment just after the facts are communicated when people add their emotional states and symbolic understanding to create a movie of what is happening. At TNT the emerging movie in the associates' minds caused them to voice questions and concerns: "What if drama is boring?" "Is drama too limiting?" "Drama can be really highbrow." "Drama is so *Masterpiece Theater.*" "Hey, we're not PBS!"

As Michael Borza remarked on the TNT video case study Boyd developed when he was part of the Tom Peters Company, "For the first three months of the meetings discussing the brand, we referred to it as the 'D' word. We were afraid to say it out loud, because we were so afraid it would have a negative connotation."

In order to put their own emotional and symbolic stamp on the Drama Club, TNT organized a corporate retreat in Florida for every single employee, another rare event. September 27, 2000, became a pivotal day in the life of TNT. "If your associates don't embrace it," said TNT's branding guru, Jennifer Dorian, "you have to trash it!"

To help them communicate and introduce the brand identity, Koonin hired the charismatic, innovative, and internationally recognized Canadian conductor Boris Brott. Brott has for years used his musical gifts to educate. His goal with TNT was to communicate the importance of playing together through music. With the respect and authority that only a maestro can command, Brott told the associates, "Only with the same song sheet can we perform in harmony." Using Beethoven's struggle for perfection as a business metaphor, he related Ludwig's career, played his music, and then taught the entire staff of TNT to play "Ode to Joy" with tone bars.

Imagine the difficulty of teaching two hundred people to play the same song, with harmony, in one short session. "It was an exciting and unifying moment," Koonin said. The meeting ended with TNT's leaders handing out sheet music inked with TNT's new brand positioning and defining the elements of drama. Every employee returned to the network's Atlanta headquarters knowing what brand tune they had to play. The message was powerful and clear. "I am the conductor," Koonin said, "and we all need to play off the same song sheet." Listed on the song sheet were attributes to help associates find the drama that "makes you think and feel."

The team created an easy way to identify the new personality they were becoming with simply stated brand ideas.

TNT is not:	TNT is:	TNT is not:
Juvenile	Contemporary	Old Fashioned
Mindless	Meaningful	Elitist
Predictable	Suspenseful	Dull
Frivolous	Exciting	Slow
Superficial	Powerful	Self-important
Sit-coms	Drama	Documentaries

This Florida retreat was held nearly ten months before TNT launched its new brand—before TNT had a tagline, new logo, or a new advertising campaign. Passionately aligned to the new promise, everyone worked the next ten months back in Atlanta preparing for the brand launch despite budget cuts, layoffs, and a terrible ad market. Ideas percolated, decisions were made, and creative plans came alive. But passion faced reality when programming began to take its cues from the new Drama Club positioning.

TNT's number one rated show at the time was *WCW Monday Nitro.* It frequently held the top position as the week's highest-rated program on basic cable. Produced by Turner Broadcasting's World Championship Wrestling, the show was a spectacle of hard bodies, screaming fans, bikini-clad dancers, and fireworks. Wrestling was a juvenile, frivolous, mindless, and sweaty 240-pound muscle-bound symbol of everything the network was not going to be.

Scot Safon was a big fan of the new brand positioning, but he expressed what others felt. "The notion that we can be a drama brand while still keeping WCW on the schedule is, well, I mean, who are we kidding?" An industry veteran, he knew that networks just don't cancel their top-rated show.

TNT did.

Scot had a conversion moment. "That was our top-rated show by more than double anything else, and we dumped it! Can you name another network that cancelled its top-rated show? I don't know if consumers noticed that we dropped wrestling from our schedule, but it said everything to the staff."

As Koonin put it, "Short-term ratings can be seductive, but we are in this for the long term."

Tuesday, June 12, 2001, was chosen as brand launch day. Everyone gathered in one of Turner's cavernous studios for D-Day (Drama Day). TNT's new logo and tagline were unveiled. Following the live on-air introduction of the new logo, a three-minute advertisement asking the question "What is drama?" premiered. It showcased Whoopi Goldberg, Dennis Hopper, Joan Allen, and other Hollywood stars celebrating drama. The message was clear, simple, and impossible to miss: "TNT: We Know Drama."

That night kicked off TNT's new programming, on-air packaging, and a three-month media plan to tout the network's new brand promise as a destination for dramatic entertainment. By their one-year anniversary, the results were astounding. TNT had become cable's number one destination for drama and had seen double-digit growth in key demographics. TNT grew 50 percent in the 2001–2002 broadcast season-to-date among adults 18 to 49 with household incomes of $75,000 plus. Because of its strong lineup of dramatic movies, TNT has become the most-watched and highest-rated basic cable network in weekend prime time for not only the 18-to-49-year-olds, but also viewers 18 to 34 and 25 to 54. This trend has generally held through the past several years. Communicating on the factual channel is easy in the cable TV business. "We are lucky," Koonin said, "to be in a business where we get a report card every day."

Creativity exploded across the network as associates embraced the new brand. "For us," Koonin said, "branding went from a buzzword to a lifestyle." This transformation was acquired by Koonin's insistence on a data-driven culture, partnered with an emotional passion to understand what that data means. This led TNT's lifestyle to include a variety of activities. Inspired by their "What is drama?" advertising spots, TNT's on-air department created internal spots showcasing associates talking about "what is dramatic about working at TNT." The answers ranged from "finding a parking space" to "working with great people."

It was in the hallways and in the work. "Morale is high, and even our meetings have become dramatic," Koonin said. One of the brand's best measures of success is the associate backlash he gets when suggesting something that's "off brand."

"We had a competition in our on-air department to identify the attributes of drama," Koonin said. Victory in the competition earned the person behind the winning idea a chance to produce a commercial featuring the attribute. Several great ideas were generated, from the drama of eating to the drama of flying. However, the winning idea featured the drama of crying. Kleenex signed on immediately to sponsor a weekly "tear jerker" movie on TNT.

Other advertisers lined up. Johnson & Johnson collaborated with TNT to create a series of original television movies that celebrate the triumph of the human spirit. Hollywood movie studios paid TNT to attach stars like Meg Ryan, Hugh Jackman, and Denzel Washington to the "What is drama?" campaign as a way to promote the studio's movies. That's like Michael Jordan paying Hanes to pitch underwear.

With the clandestine work of only three associates, TNT organized the first annual Drammy's. This internal award program bestowed prizes on associates for the "Most Dramatic Moment," "Most Dramatic Celebrity Encounter," and "Most Dramatic email." The award for the "Most Dramatic Meeting" went to the pregnant vice president of branding, whose water broke during a staff meeting. Jennifer Dorian, now called the "Drama Mama," gave birth to daughter Claudia the next day. If emotional communication can be measured by associates keeled over in laughter and literally peeing in their pants, then Koonin accomplished his objective.

TNT's Drammy's culminated in the crowning of a "Drama King" and "Drama Queen." Scot Safon was the inaugural Drama King at TNT. Safon said that as he looked back at all the work that went into the branding initiative, he could see the three channels of communication altering everything. "Everything was backed by the facts. Steve put an emotional overlay on it. Symbols were deployed."

Ask Steve Koonin how important communicating in facts, emotions, and symbols was to the success of TNT's branding initiative, and he'll give you a one-word response in his usual dramatic fashion.

"HUGE!"

The Gift of Sight

Vision Exam, Phase I

Before LensCrafters existed, buying a new pair of glasses involved making an appointment with a doctor to obtain a prescription, waiting several days or weeks for the prescription to be filled at a remotely located lab, and then returning to your doctor for a fitting. Grinding the lenses took only about an hour at the lab, but the inefficient system required an unnecessarily long waiting period. Americans hate to wait.[2]

Seeing a potential reversal of this waiting period, LensCrafters brought labs and doctors together in one place and reduced the wait to about an hour. The first LensCrafters opened in Florence, Kentucky, in 1983, but before long there was a second, third, and fourth store. The one-hour concept caught on quickly with busy consumers. From its beginning, LensCrafters was a company driven by an entrepreneur's dream and an innovator's heart. By the second year, dozens of locations were opened and the company had established its guiding vision and values. During the spring of 1986 two stores were opening per week, and by 1988, just five years after its inception, LensCrafters had 278 stores in the United States. By 2007 there were more than 875 retail locations operating in the United States, Canada, and Puerto Rico.

Vision Exam, Phase II

However, like many companies with a soaring start, it began to plateau. Ban Hudson, LensCrafters' highly regarded leader during this first phase, moved to become CEO of U.S. Shoe, LensCrafters' parent company. Ban tapped Dave Browne to be his successor. A brash thirty-year-old executive, Browne was charged with taking LensCrafters to the next level.

For a company with such an amazingly successful start, this was no small task. Dave Browne was one of those unique individuals who glows with success and confidence and grabbed the challenge with zeal. He was brilliant when it came to financial analysis, retail operations, and marketplace leverage. Like an MBA on steroids, he brought the discipline of steel-trap analysis to a hardworking gang of passionate mavericks. He was competitive and needed to win. Browne was the kind of executive that Wall Street loves.

However, he was also a self-proclaimed "numbers-only butthead." Browne's primary problem was that he relied too much on the factual channel. Those around him appreciated his genius and respected him, but it was clear that although he was the CEO and the boss, he was not the leader of the company. It's one of those unfortunate side effects that often come along with analytical brilliance accompanied with less-than-average emotional intelligence. He was unable to inspire people to the next level, because he was dealing only in facts. "I knew every detail," he said. He was trapped in the factual channel mantra of better, faster, cheaper.

While LensCrafters needed to look inward to improve efficiency and productivity, the company and Dave Browne were struggling to provide any reason beyond facts for associates to change. "I only talked about the head, never the heart," Browne told us. We watched as a gutsy company full of passion and pride began to look more like a best practices machine. While sales began to increase, passion and alignment began to fade. People made the numbers, but the numbers didn't stand for much besides score keeping.

We watched as he struggled to incorporate negative upward feedback. He began to feel the loss of company spirit he had enjoyed during Hudson's tenure and became personally concerned that maybe he had played a part in drowning the heart of an enterprise with data. Browne realized that he needed to change. "I needed to transform LensCrafters by transforming myself," he said. Wanting to rejuvenate the company's spirit, he pulled together a group of key LensCrafters associates to rework a vision as a prelude to their tenth-anniversary celebration. After much hard work, they called it the Decade II Vision, Mission, and Core Values. The new vision was to "be the best at helping the world see." They wanted to be the best by "delivering legendary customer service" and by "developing and energizing associates and leaders in the world's best workplace." They also wanted to help the "world see by being conveniently available to people everywhere," being the "first choice for eye care." However, the symbolic centerpiece of the vision was summed up in LensCrafters' promise of "giving the gift of sight to those who have the least and need us the most." In Browne's own words, "The Gift of Sight program was the key to bringing more heart into the business."

While everyone knew Browne had approved the work that went into the vision and Gift of Sight program, no one really knew how deeply he cared about it until the day of the tenth-anniversary celebration in March 1993. A huge tent had been set up behind the headquarters building, where the typical corporate festivities were in swing. Browne took center stage to address his associates, as he had many times before. But this day was different. He had ended his soul searching. To add to the emotion, LensCrafters had just passed Pearle Vision to become the world's largest super-optical, and a well-regarded associate was critically ill in the hospital.

On this day Browne did not stand and recite the numbers; instead, he related a personal story. He recounted growing up on the streets of Philadelphia during some hard times. He let people know the principles that his immigrant father, who was in the audience, had inspired. "My dad made sacrifices for me" he said. "He's been working as a mechanic at the same job his whole life." He told us that he was thinking about his faith and family and that he realized he didn't have to be the stereotypical "Wall Street CEO." Browne said, "I still wanted to win; I just wanted to win with heart." When he was finished speaking, he received a standing ovation. It was not the obligatory applause of deference, but the applause of associates who were showing their appreciation for their leader as well as their boss.

As Dave Browne spread the news of the Decade II Vision, Mission, and Core Values, he began to communicate the symbolism of the "gift of sight" with more emotion. His metaphor was simple: "Take the high ground before all others." He said the company was absolutely committed to treating everyone right. "We weren't going to cheat associates, bait and switch customers, or sell through trivial promotions. We were going to take the high ground." And though the symbol was simple, the emotions were genuine. The people at LensCrafters began to feel the change.

The Gift of Sight program provides eye exams and eyewear free of charge to the poor. It was especially important to Browne. Realizing its importance to everyone else, he shifted his former posture that communicated huge confidence to others. "I said 'yes' and got out of the way." Today the program has served more than 5 million underprivileged people in the United States and twenty-five developing countries around the world. Luxottica, now the parent company of

LensCrafters, has a stated goal of serving 7 million by the end of 2008.

Once Dave Browne started communicating with facts, emotions, and symbols, LensCrafters left the plateau it had become stuck upon. It has become one of the greatest niche-retail success stories ever. Browne did not stop being the MBA on steroids. He simply added the emotional and symbolic channels to his fact-based communication repertoire.

Vision Exam, Phase III

As the helicopter maneuvered through fog-enshrouded Monte Marmolada in the Southern Alps near Agordo, Italy, Dave Browne's guts churned. He wasn't as much concerned about the flight as he was about what was waiting for him on the ground. He was meeting with Leonardo Del Vecchio, whose successful hostile takeover of LensCrafters' parent company, U.S. Shoe, had made him Browne's new boss. At an early age, Del Vecchio had lost his father and was placed in an orphanage. When he was twelve he started his training as a machinist and medallion maker, skills he starting employing to fashion eyewear when he was fourteen. By the age of seventy-one, Del Vecchio had amassed such a fortune that in 2007 he was ranked on *Forbes* magazine's 100 Richest People in the World roster at number 52.

Luxottica, formerly a vendor, was now the parent company. Browne was considering what he was going to say to his ten thousand associates upon his return to the United States. Two metaphors came to his mind. "We've climbed one mountain and now have another one to climb." Looking over the blanketing fog across the valley, he thought, "If we hold hands, stick together, and keep moving, we can make it to the top of even a higher mountain."

Browne and Del Vecchio's first meetings were extremely professional and polite. Del Vecchio was gracious and patient with the leader of his newest acquisition. He knew from experience that the first steps of a relationship often determine its ultimate course. However, the two men spoke different languages, both literally and metaphorically. Luxottica was a high-fashion brand-driven company;

LensCrafters, an operation company focused by strong vision and values. Luxottica was a wholesaler and manufacturer; LensCrafters, a retailer.

Browne was determined that LensCrafters would not lose the "heart that made the company special," while Luxottica would get an exceptional return on their investment. As he talked with his associates, he communicated the symbolism of climbing mountains and navigating fog. "This metaphor helped us get through a year of uncertainty," he said. Boyd and I would add that it was Browne and his senior team's skillful use of the metaphor that helped. He told his associates that if they needed assistance, all they had to do was "hold each other's hands a little tighter." And he and his team were the role models, making themselves more available than ever for questions and concerns, and for sorting out the mixed messages that uncertain times inevitably bring.

With regard to his relationship with Del Vecchio, Browne told us, "The language and cultural differences were challenging, but, surprisingly, we first really connected at a heart level." Claudio Del Vecchio, Leonardo's son, embraced the Gift of Sight program and helped his father visualize it in terms of branding. Soon all three leaders were embracing the idea of "helping the world to see through the gift of sight." This common ground allowed them to start lifting the fog. Browne described his experience from that point onward as "the smoothest hostile take over in history."

Today Luxottica Group's mission statement reads: "We at Luxottica aim at protecting the eyes and enhancing the faces of men and women all over the world, by manufacturing and selling ophthalmic eyewear and sunwear characterized by their high technical and stylistic quality, in order to maximize our customers' well-being and satisfaction." It's a testimony that cultures can blend style with vision, brand with operations, and communicate with facts, passion, and symbolism.

5

SYMBOLS AND
STORIES

Judy S. DeLoache loves to study how children develop their cognitive abilities. In the mid-1980s she was studying toddler memory. The age of three seems to mark a shift in cognitive ability, so Judy designed a study and watched how children younger than three and just a little older than three would do with a simple task. She would take them to a dollhouse-size scale model of a typical family room. Judy would show a three-year-old a tiny plastic toy dog named "Little Snoopy." She would place Little Snoopy in a hiding place in the miniature room as the child watched. Then she would take the child to an exact life-size replica of the family room and encourage the child to find "Big Snoopy," a life-size version of the toy dog, "hiding in the same place in his big room." The three-year-olds loved the game and could easily find Big Snoopy. Children younger than three, however, could not find Big Snoopy.[1]

In a golden moment of insight (a cherished experience for all researchers), Judy, now Kenan Professor of Psychology at the University of Virginia, realized that the cognitive ability at work was not memory but the ability to understand symbols. She began to shift her research emphasis and has worked the past twenty years or so on how children develop symbolic understanding. Her conclusions are profound. "There is no domain of development more important than mastery of the various symbols and symbol systems used for communication."[2]

From a rabbit's foot to a rosary, symbols are shortcuts to the great truths that guide our lives. The ring on your finger, the blue ribbon you saved, and the flower pressed in a book all mean something. Scouts name their den, high schools choose mascots, families inherit crests, companies design logos, and nations raise flags. The stories we tell, the art we display, or the music we play symbolizes who we are. Symbols are the emblems of culture that tell us who we are and where we have been, tying generations to the same ideals.

Whether using imagery-rich language, elegant formulas, or supporting images, symbols are part of our lives. Our research shows that when leaders are communicating at the top of their game (notice the metaphor), they fill the symbolic channel using symbols or language that are pertinent to the audience. Relying on familiar metaphors or fresh word pictures, leaders who possess effective communication skills are able to stimulate the symbolic channel in a way that supports the factual and emotional channel to create a compelling movie. Vast and complicated neurological systems create and manipulate symbols and symbolic language. We will limit our considerations primarily to metaphors and stories, with a few asides along the way.

A symbol is as powerful as the action or emotion it evokes. We attach more symbols to things that are more important. Win a volleyball tournament and a trophy symbolizes athletic victory. Graduation tassels, gowns, and diplomas signify years of scholastic achievement. Wedding vows, veils, rings, garters, bouquets, toasts, broken glasses, things borrowed, and things blue celebrate the promise of love and commitment. Symbols are as natural as smiles, shrugs, and winks. They are communication shortcuts that do the heavy lifting for both the sender and the receiver. They convey mutual understanding and individual meaning at the same time.

Types of Symbols

The following is a short list of the kinds of symbols, actions, or symbolic language we use to refer to symbolic ideas.

Logos, word pictures, stories, anecdotes, myths, metaphors, legends, analogies, slogans, mottos, quotations, poems, creeds, examples, pictures, similes, parables, designs, equations, charts, graphs, colors, artifacts, lists, traditions, customs, shrines, insignias, celebrations, awards, perks, praises, ceremonies, rituals, heroes, music, theme songs, statues, certificates, organizational structures, flags, architectural blueprints, models.

Applying symbols to corporate brands is a challenging and rewarding task. Shapes like Coca-Cola's bottle, Nike's swoosh, or McDonalds' golden arches are brand emblems. Colors, too, are important brand elements, like *National Geographic's* yellow border, UPS's brown trucks and uniforms, the color pink for breast cancer awareness, and Orange's, uh, orange. Rolls-Royce, Louis Vuitton, Virgin, M&Ms, Amazon, FedEx, Flickr, and Google use stylized text to symbolize their brand. Ralph Lauren has its polo player. Gateway has its cowhide. Mercedes has its three-pointed star. Apple has it's, uh, apple. The Tata Group uses a combination of symbols—an emblem, stylized text, and the color blue—to convey the idea of fluidity, although some people have interpreted the logo as representing a tree while others see mirror-image waterfalls.

Enduring Symbols

Some symbols seem to last as long as Mother Nature and Father Time. The phrase "hang out" was very popular in the 1830s. It referred to the custom of socializing in the neighborhood where your or your group's trade shingle was hung. Today's expression "hanging in the 'hood" might be a redundant reconstruction of this original idea. The term "big cheese" is an interpretation of the Urdu word chiz, meaning "thing." As this word traveled from colonial India to Britain, it became attached to the idea of "something good." By the twentieth century, the term "big cheese" referred to the head of an organization or other powerful figure, whether that person was good or not. Saint Augustine, circa 397 ce, consulted Saint Ambrose as to which day was the correct day to fast. Ambrose said, "When I am at Rome, I fast on a Saturday; when I am at Milan, I do not. Follow the custom of the church where you are." In 1621 Robert Burton, scholar and vicar at Oxford University, rephrased this statement as "When they are at Rome, they do there as they see done," in his *The Anatomy of Melancholy*. Eventually this became the more familiar phrase, "When in Rome, do as the Romans do."[3]

Others have shorter shelf lives. The 1990 Kodak annual report displayed a white-water rafting trip. The symbolism of "perpetual white-water" was not lost on employees and investors. While it worked okay, the white-water symbol lacked the power of originality, as this metaphor was in common usage at the time. The hair-loss product Rogaine also used white-water rapids to explain the perils of hair loss. One of their commercials from this era depicted balding men bonding on a river-raft trip. Repeated usage during a short time frame may fatigue symbols, eroding their effectiveness. It's like telling a too-familiar joke. Or having only one joke.

Using a familiar symbol in a new context, however, can provide fresh meaning. Before World War I, a young Captain Douglas MacArthur needed to communicate his plan to use the National Guard in battle to President Woodrow Wilson. At that time the Civil War was as fresh in people's minds as the Persian Gulf War is today. Veterans of the Civil War still marched in parades and spoke to the young guardsmen who served. Each individual state had deep ties to its National Guard units.

Practically speaking, however, the Civil War had been over for fifty years. The states had relaxed their demands on the National Guard, resulting in units that lacked leadership, training, and experience. To fix this, the War Department wanted the National Guard units completely integrated into the regular army. Theirs was a controversial and unpopular proposal.

Captain MacArthur presented a different idea to the White House. He affirmed that the citizen soldiers of the National Guard were an important part of America's democracy. He was against the wholesale integration of the guard units into the regular army. So he proposed creating a division of the army, populated by troops from each state, that would "stretch over the country like a rainbow." Regular army officers would command and train this division, and all states would be proudly represented. President Wilson adopted MacArthur's plan, and the great 42nd Rainbow Division was born. They fought with distinction throughout World War I.

The Power of Metaphor

"Language is, indeed, the ultimate symbolic mental function, and it is virtually impossible to conceive of thought as we know it in its absence," declares Ian Tattersall, curator in the Department of Anthropology of the American Museum of Natural History in New York City.[4] Steve Mithen, of the University of Reading's Department of Archeology, suggests that symbolic abilities are part of the evolutionary transition from prehistoric to modern man, saying, "[T]he transition from Neanderthal man to Cro-Magnon is marked precisely by the ability to 'switch cognitive frames': the Paleolithic blossoming in art may be correlated with the ability to think metaphorically."[5] George Lakoff, professor of linguistics at the University of California at Berkeley, goes very far in his thesis that our ability to use metaphor and other symbolic language is a powerful and everyday form of our cognitive abilities. "Expressions like wasting time, attacking positions, going our separate ways, etc., are reflections of systematic metaphorical concepts that structure our actions and thoughts. The are 'alive' in the most fundamental sense: they are metaphors we live by."[6]

Scientists who often desperately try to avoid metaphor find doing so extraordinarily difficult. Steven Pinker, formerly with M.I.T. and now Johnstone Family Professor in the Department of Psychology at Harvard University, says, "Even the most recondite scientific reasoning is an assembly of down-home mental metaphors."[7] Susan Oyama, sometimes dubbed as a philosopher of biology, is an outspoken proponent of using great rigor when constructing scientific thoughts and the effect of metaphor upon these constructs. I usually need a dictionary close at hand when reading her work, but she works hard at helping scientists understand how metaphor influences how they frame scientific inquiry. Concerning metaphor and the choice of her book title, *Evolution's Eye,* she wrote, "To be sure, scientific metaphors involve not just ways of talking and writing, but ways of seeing and doing. They are implicated in the practices of research, form the initial direction of attention right on to the interpretation, promulgation of results, and application. My choice of title reflects a conviction that one cannot talk about matters of theory and practice without attending to the nuances of language."[8]

Common Metaphors

From sunup to sundown, we are asked for examples of symbolic language. Communicating symbolically is as natural as breathing, but like fish in water, sometimes it is so familiar we don't know it exists. To illustrate, let's take a moment to have some fun. Read the the metaphor-filled paragraphs below, and insert your industry name, organization's name, senior executive's name, or other personal reference where indicated by brackets. So take a spin, try it on for size, and see how it sits with you. Once you soak up some of these ideas, we are sure you'll be able to wring out your own.

Ever since the bubble burst, the [_____] industry went into a fiery free fall, exploding as it hit rock bottom. It's a jungle out there. It's like constant whitewater. You know, a real roller-coaster ride. This is no easy row to hoe—some days it's like pushing a rope uphill—but hey, play the hand you're dealt and go with the flow. We're walking tightropes this time, on the razor's edge, no margin for error, no safety net, a lead-lined parachute, and the edge is thin ice.

We better move fast because [_____] has a bee in his bonnet, ants in his pants, and is on the warpath again. Fail and there will be hell to pay, leaving us all out in the cold. Working for [_____] is the blind leading the blind. We can't see the forest for the trees, and we have that sense of déjà vu all over again. This is a real seat-of-the-pants operation. My [_____] is lost in the fog. I wish they would wake up and smell the (coffee, river, roses, inspiration, denial, etc.) already.

A year ago we were on top of the world, but today we have the weight of the world on our shoulders, up the creek without a paddle. [_____], we have a problem. We're juggling a million priorities, wading through mountains of red tape, and just trying to keep our heads above water. Our hands are tied, we've got a gag order, and we're hoping the creek don't rise. Were carrying those jerks over in [_____] on our backs. The ball and chain at our desks was replaced with golden handcuffs, and now those have turned to tin. Strategy is really screwed up, stinks to high heaven, is full of holes, DOA; all the king's men can't put it back together. Where's the duct tape when you need it? Call in the cavalry.

My [_____] keeps saying to pick up the pace, raise the bar, pull out all the stops, set our sights, and shoot for the moon. It's time for us to kick butt and take names, take the hill, spank the competition. Geronimo! We better get on board, the train is leaving the station; seat backs and tray tables in their upright and locked positions, switch off all electronic devices, buckle up, and keep your hands and head inside the ride at all times. We've crossed the Rubicon, need to burn the boats, and ignore the sirens' call. If it crashes, we'll be left holding the bag, and that'll be a dark day. Elvis has left the building.

There is a pot of gold at the end of the rainbow, and we're headed for the promised land, always chasing the brass ring. I'm talking touchdown, hat trick, double doubles. There's light at the end of the tunnel, and its all downhill from here. I get the lowdown on the down low. Hate to break your crayons, but you've been phished dry.

These examples address three powerful points about metaphors. First, metaphors are natural communication constructs. They will fly out of your mouth or march from your keyboard, intended or not. Second, most metaphors are culturally absorbed constructs, so even though they may be useful, they are limited by the cultural contexts in which they are used. And third, even common, everyday metaphors convey structure, establish a framework for reasoning or decision making, and structure the language we use to indicate to others how we think about matters.

To illustrate the first point, I remember an interaction I had with Group Health during a communication workshop I was facilitating. We had just completed a few exercises on how to play with metaphors and select those that best represent a leader's message. This kind of work is easy for some and more difficult for others. At the end of the exercise, one of the participants raised her hand and said with serious concern, "Ron, I just don't think I can pull metaphors out of my sleeve at the drop of a hat." After the laughter subsided in the room, we had a great discussion about how metaphor shapes our language.

When I read scholarly research, metaphors often peek through the more technically (and sometimes awkwardly) constructed sentences researchers use. Take this bit of text, for example:

> Over the course of our lives, the requirements for spoken communication foster selectivity in metaphors, forcing us more frequently to use metaphors that have cultural currency so that their meaning will be intersubjectively shared with those to whom we talk, and they will hence be useful in clarifying our point. Some experiences may be widely shared by members of a national culture, while other experiences may be limited to members of a restricted group, such as members of an organizational culture.[9]

Notice how this quotation about metaphors uses the metaphors of "currency" and "clarifying" to make its point. The currency metaphor refers to how these structures of speech act as forms of exchanges that have value, just as currency does. The clarifying metaphor is used in the same way a chef clarifies butter. Heating butter lets water evaporate and separates the milk solids from the fat. The more refined liquid fat is what the chef wants—it is what is essential. The authors of the above quote wanted to indicate that they were getting to the essential parts.

This research quote illustrates the second point about metaphors—that their acquisition is hugely influenced by the cultures in which they are learned. Every person lives within multiple cultures, ranging from national, commercial, religious, political, organizational, "pop," and familial. So metaphors are inherited or acquired from many sources. Some of these sources are very particular to a distinct group—we often hear someone trying to explain an idiom from another language, and sometimes it translates well and sometimes it doesn't. Some cultures, like the global culture of business, develop metaphorical references that are widely understood. The skilled leader will not only use these more universal metaphors, but will also learn a few metaphors from a variety of cultures in order to connect better with others.

And the third point about everyday metaphors has been reviewed in great detail by various researchers. Whether the metaphors are structural, procedural, spatial, conceptual, orientational, or something else, they are born from an experiential basis. That's why we experience their effect every day, because metaphors are the communication vehicles that represent how we actually live. Consider the simple example of how we use the common, everyday business metaphor "time is money."

You are wasting my precious time.

This gadget will save you hours.

I don't have time to invest in this idea.

We need to budget our time to get this project completed.

The merger was successful, but we're still living on borrowed time.

Thanks for your time.

My time is up.

Stop wasting time and get to the point.

Metaphorical Depth

Using a rainbow as a symbol of unification has many modern appearances. The term "rainbow coalition" can refer to any of the following groups: the Kenyan National Rainbow Coalition political party, the Canadian Rainbow Health Coalition, and the Rainbow/PUSH coalition, which is a merger of Jesse Jackson's National Rainbow Coalition and PUSH (People United to Save Humanity). The rainbow metaphor stems from the idea that light is composed of many colors, and the fact that this metaphor is commonly used does not necessarily diminish its effectiveness. However, the idea of a rainbow is most often used metaphorically as a one-dimensional comparison—the idea of many from one source or many things coming together as one.

Metaphors can work at this one-to-one comparison level, and most of the time when evoked in day-to-day usage they convey only a simple comparison. The strength of this type of comparison can be profound. Boyd used to tell a story about a meeting at a hospital system where the CEO regaled his audience of senior managers with a bullet-by-bullet overview of all the factual data concerning the hospital's need to grow, especially through acquisition. It was a masterful display of data, and the emotional output was businesslike but sincere. As the meeting concluded, one of the senior managers was discussing the meeting with her subordinates and said, "I know he's right, but cancer grows, too." The injection of this simple one-to-one cautionary metaphor elicited more commentary than the CEO's recitation.

A classic political example of the effective use of metaphor comes from John F. Kennedy's famous July 26, 1963, speech in Berlin. He wanted to connect an old phrase with a new phrase to cement the earnestness of his political devotion to freedom. Speaking from the Schöneberg city hall to a crowd with their backs pressed against the Berlin Wall, he said, "Two thousand years ago the proudest boast was *civis Romanus sum*. Today, in the world of freedom, the proudest boast is 'Ich bin ein Berliner.'" Connecting "I am a Roman" with "I am a Berliner" was a historical metaphor recast in a contemporary setting. Kennedy added this idea to his speech shortly before he delivered it, seeking linguistic help from his interpreter, Robert Lochner, so that he would pronounce the German phrase properly. The persisting urban legend that the audience at the time thought Kennedy had proclaimed himself to be a jelly donut (a popular pastry at the time was known as a Berliner) is fun but incorrect. The truth is, the speech was considered one of Kennedy's finest. Linguist Jürgen Eichhoff, in one scholarly report, stated, "'Ich bin ein Berliner' is not only correct but the one and only correct way of expressing in German what the President intended to say."[10]

Metaphors can create multiple connections between one idea and another. This is both a strength and a weakness. As a communicator, if you haven't thought about the multiple levels of interpretation that exist when using a metaphor, you can be burned. You can mean one thing and others may immediately seize on a different interpretation, with unfortunate results. The cancer story above is one example of this experience. The power of a metaphor comes with practicing the idea well enough that you know the extent of its various connections and can use them well. All metaphorical comparisons break down at some point. As a communicator, you should know in advance where the breakdowns may occur so that you can avoid them.

Jim Ashton is chief executive officer for SunGard's Financial Systems division. In 2005 SunGard went private in order to restructure for a future IPO. Ashton was working overtime with his team, trying to help them understand the time constraints of their strategy. He wanted to use a familiar car race metaphor to create an analogy to SunGard's situation. After considering the full extent of the metaphor, he modified the idea of a race to the entire production of winning, from pit crews, racecar engineering, and even the strategy of pit stops. His annual message was a resounding success, as the multilayered metaphor had more clout than a single-layer metaphor.

Metaphorical Actions

Saint or sinner, a leader's actions symbolically convey values, vision, and strategy. Gandhi is the quintessential exemplar. He walked to the sea to make salt, and he spent an hour a day at a spinning wheel. His goal, however, was neither to manufacture salt nor weave his own clothes, but to symbolize India's desire to self-govern. Churchill used a parlor trick to symbolize his disagreement. He often pushed a long pin through the center of a cigar. When an adversary took the podium in Parliament, Churchill would light this cigar. All eyes eventually riveted on the growing length of cigar ash, which distracted the politicians from the speaker. Southwest Airlines' Herb Kelleher once rode his Harley into a meeting to signify the company's daring spirit. In fact, Kelleher is unabashed at public displays that showcase the idea of having fun while working. For Halloween 2007, he dressed up as Dr. Derek "McDreamy" Shepherd of ABC's *Grey's Anatomy*.[11] Ted Turner strolled the old CNN newsroom in his bathrobe, exemplifying his eccentric and novel approach to business. Each of these acts added dimension to the story of these leaders.

The legendary Charles Kettering invented the electric cash register for NCR in 1905, improved automobile ignition systems in 1908, and in 1912 supplied the auto industry's first electric starter for Cadillac through his start-up, Delco. He believed in the inventive capabilities of collaboration and often used phrases like "The Wright brothers flew right through the smoke screen of impossibility" to communicate his ideas.[12] By 1920 he was General Motors' research director, where he worked for twenty-seven years, but not all of his inventions were in the automotive industry. He also developed a treatment for sexually transmitted disease and an incubator for premature infants. He was one of the industrialists who helped sponsor and organize the cancer research center that bears his name, the Memorial Sloan-Kettering Cancer Center.

Kettering lived in Dayton, Ohio, and commuted to Detroit. He often bragged that he could make the trip in less than four hours, besting all other executives. His secret was to travel side roads that bypassed the traffic-clogged city centers of Route 25. One day an executive colleague traveled with him, complaining to Kettering, "You aren't taking the normal route." This led the executive to learn the secret to one of Kettering's sayings: "You never get anywhere going the obvious way. If you want to get anything done in this world, get off Route 25."[13]

Metaphors Reveal a Leader's Mind

One of the most determined and strong-minded executives Boyd and I ever worked for had a terrific way with words. He would encapsulate complexity with simple metaphorical statements and could rouse an audience to want to perform. The basic theme he stroked time and again was winning against the undeserving and evil competitors, for at the time we started working with this executive, his division was way behind in the international rankings. The goal was the standard, obvious business goal: become number one. And the metaphorical rants that worked the best for this leader—at least for a time—were based in warfare. He used the imagery of littering the streets with the dead bodies of hapless competitors, and this same imagery was echoed throughout his division by many of his managers. It was high-testosterone stuff.

But as the division began to gain and surpass some of its competitors and the overall company began to broaden its goals, the warfare theme ran a bit stale and wasn't as useful anymore. Unfortunately for the executive, it was how he really felt, and changing metaphors to match the mood and times was difficult for him. As George Lakoff and Mark Johnson explain, "Because we reason in terms of metaphor, the metaphors we use determine a great deal about how we live our lives."[14] For this executive, competition was a real and ultimately worthy goal, and the idea of going to war with the competition worked for him. It just didn't work for everyone else all the time.

A leader needs to do two things when it comes to using metaphors. First, use the ones that come naturally to you. These will have more credibility, since they reflect your real state of mind. Second, take a look at the way you refer to things, and ask yourself if this is how you really feel, if it is what you really mean, and if it is the best expression for connecting with the circumstances you face. Expanding your metaphorical range provides you with two powerful advantages: first, it will lead you to literally think differently about your organizational issues; and second, it will allow you a greater range of expression. And as you develop a greater range, you may find more power. As Ted Kooser, thirteenth poet laureate of the United States suggests, "Metaphor conveys a confidence and certainty that in turn characterizes the speaker."[15]

Allow your metaphorical references to truly represent your best mind about everyday matters and matters of great consequence.

The Power of Stories

Stories explain the unexplainable. Every culture has used stories to explain why the sun comes up each morning, why the weather changes, how commercial markets operate, and where loved ones go when they die. Myth, tradition, morality, and religious stories teach children complexities in ways they can understand. Parables are time-honored story forms that are fanciful on the outside but reveal a great truth on the inside.

"Telling stories precedes language, since it is, in fact, a condition for language," says Antonio Damasio. His investigations led him to the conclusion that storytelling is a neurological phenomenon requiring sources that are scattered throughout the brain.[16] The ability to generate narratives stems from the brain's ability to integrate a great many functions from both hemispheres, from different lobes (spatial and temporal), and from the mid-brain (hippocampus) to the cerebral cortex. The complexity of this integration allows us to have a storytelling ability that "Lets us see for ourselves, and share with others, the fundamental way in which our minds come to integrate experience."[17]

It appears that people are born with the ability to tell stories. Oral storytelling traditions have a far longer history than written stories. Many researchers reviewing the history of oral traditions have found that storytelling is more than just an art—it is a method of conveying cultural history over time. While cultural storytellers can reinterpret stories and change them for their own purposes, these oral histories can sometimes pass from generation to generation with great fidelity. Even today there are communities with no established written language that convey their history via storytelling from one generation to the next. For example, the Fang live in the hot, humid, equatorial rain forests of equatorial Africa, in the political boundaries known as Cameroon, Guinea, and Gabon (where they represent well more than half the population). Leadership in the Fang culture is inherited along family lines in much the same way as is experienced throughout the world. The leader serves as the spiritual leader, able to communicate with the ancestors of the village. He wears masks, which Fang are famous for, during these communications.

Pascal Boyer is Henry Luce Professor of Individual and Collective Memory at Washington University in St. Louis, Missouri. He has studied Fang storytelling and found that the Fang consider recalling and retelling stories prestigious. "Many Fang people take particular pride in being able to recall very long stories in precise detail. Such people, traditional storytellers, often challenge others to recall what happened at what point in this or that story."[18]

Contrast this ability with reading and writing. Others have to teach you to read and write, and you use different brain systems for this activity than you use for natural storytelling. Reading and writing can aid storytelling but are not a requirement for it. A great deal has been written about storytelling and how managers need to become better at it. The ability to tell a story well means using the story to convey important ideas with simple structures. Stories are the easiest forms to help others understand complexity, as long as the stories are well crafted and communicated in a manner that conveys the intentions of the leader. I once reported up through a chain of managers to an executive who had wonderful storytelling abilities. He would often regale a large audience with homespun stories about his bucolic childhood. As we listened, my colleagues and I actually strained to hear the message contained in the story. We debated what he was driving toward. But there was no message. This executive could tell a good story, but could not make it apply to anything about our business. Some of my colleagues referred to him as "the suit with nobody in it."

What Stories Do

An easy way to think about how we learn is to divide the world of experience into two parts—what we learn from direct experience, and what we learn indirectly from all other sources. A great number of these lessons, especially those that stick, generate story-like explanations in our minds that we recall and use on a continuous basis.

While there are many artful approaches to storytelling, the fundamentals concerning what the story does are also simple. A story can do one of three things. First, it can work like Velcro by attaching a vivid example to the main idea the leader is asking a group to consider. The Velcro metaphor for stories is familiar but useful. Velcro works by mashing together two strips of material. One side is a bunch of loops, and the other side a bunch of hooks. When mashed together, the hooks slip into the loops and the sides stick together. The density of hooks and loops, as well as the materials used, changes Velcro's strength.

A second thing a story can do is instruct, guide, debate, or refer to actions that the leader and others need to take. These are the stories of caution, morality, business savvy, innovation, purpose, and so forth that are used to help a leader's central movie remain alive. Even case studies are just a stuffy way of telling a story. Chapter 3 covered the ideas of refining and retelling a central movie while keeping the movie updated. This second kind of story helps with this process a great deal. A customer service complaint that a leader encounters in the morning can become a story that illustrates one of the leader's themes that same afternoon—themes such as the need for good service, the process of how good service is provided, how customer service establishes market share, or how living out the true intentions of customer service helps make work rewarding.

The third possibility for a story is that it may both reveal something and stick to a main idea (like the central movie) at the same time. This is a powerful story method and not that difficult to master. In any case, stories need to be easy enough to understand but interesting enough to hold attention. As Robin Hogarth, a professor at Universitat Pompeu Fabra's Barcelona Graduate School of Economics, suggests in his work on how to develop intuition: "The speed and ease of understanding achieved through stories depend on your being able to see immediately the resemblance between aspects of the story and (your) reality. At the same time, elements of the story create links with different parts of your memory and thereby engage further connections in your mind. In other words, through similarity, a story can make many links with the mind, something a more explicit, rational explanation cannot do."[19]

Stories explain what charts and tables of data often cannot. They provide an answer the symbolic system is looking for—an answer couched in terms that are different from those that satisfy the factual system. And if the story—whether literally true or allegorical—helps the data come alive through narrative, then your movie will be more complete and likely more compelling.

3-D Storytelling

One approach to crafting stories is 3D-Storytelling, an easy-to-remember process Boyd and I came up with. Stories need detail, dialogue, and drama to be effective. These three D's turn flat, ordinary stories into three-dimensional stories that will either strengthen the Velcro power of a story, provide a better instruction basis for the story, or add the really sticky stickiness of Velcro plus instruction.

When it comes to relating the details of a story, it is important to consider the number, the kind, and the order. Do you know someone who relates each and every miscellaneous detail of a story whether it matters or not? And what is your response when you listen to such a rambling, ineffectual retelling? Our suggestion is, don't include too many details in your own storytelling. Instead, think about your story ahead of time and figure out which details are important for the occasion. The same story can have many, many details, but certain ones will take the stage for different occasions. Also consider the kinds of details that would most interest and match the audience. While many business stories don't require too much editing in terms of audience, being sensitive to the interests of your audience will strengthen your communication. Finally, figure out which details come first, second, or third. Sometimes a leader can use this simple idea of order to establish a parallel argument with the point the story is illustrating.

Dialogue is essential to effective storytelling, because it moves a story from a simple description of events to the narration or reliving of the event. When someone in the story speaks, it helps the audience understand that a real event is being replayed for their consideration. It shows rather than tells the relationships between the people, organizations, or even ideas that the story is conveying. Narration depends on dialogue, and when people experience a narrative, they are not just hearing a description of prior events, but are drawn into the reliving of these events. Of course, a certain level of embellishment is permissible in these recounts, but the best stories are those that are true. Barry Lopez has been the Welch Professor of American Studies at the University of Notre Dame, has taught fiction at the Bread Loaf Writers' Conference, and travels regularly to Texas Tech University, where he is the university's Visiting Distinguished Scholar. He suggests that as long as the storyteller "uses his storytelling skill to heighten and emphasize certain relationships, it is even possible for the story to be more successful than the storyteller himself is able to imagine."[20]

Drama can mean many different things. "Effective stories have drama … the drama centers on the storyteller's need to make tough choices, usually without perfect information or the complete alignment of the stakeholders involved."[21] This is one form of drama. We think of drama as the form of impact you intend for your story to take. Is this a cautionary tale, a story of resilience, a happy story, a sad story, or a story that starts woefully but ends with relief? The dramatic impact of the story depends on how you intend to use it. Some stories are humorous by nature, yet in addition to simply being amusing, humor can be used to uplift, instill an element of sobriety, or make a sensitive issue more accessible.

The list that follows offers just some of the typical occasions or opportunities for leaders to use storytelling in addition to or independently of any metaphorical structure to their message. Using 3D-Storytelling can greatly enhance the effectiveness of any of these stories.

Identity story: Who am I?

Purpose story: Why are we here?

Foresight story: Where are we going? How will we get there?

Conflict story: How do we deal with conflict?

Negotiation story: How will I negotiate?

Reorganization story: Why are we changing?

Inspiration story: Why should we press on?

Problem-solving story: How will we figure this out?

Thematic story: How does this help explain a theme?

Sample Stories

Marilyn Carlson Nelson is the chair and CEO of Carlson Companies, Inc., which owns such brands as Radisson Hotels, Seven Seas Cruises, T.G.I.Friday's, and Carlson Travel. When Marilyn was speaking at a diversity conference at the College of St. Benedict, a women's college in St. Joseph, Minnesota, she wanted to make a point about the importance of personal responsibility, initiative, and resolve. She used a wonderful, first-person Velcro type of story to illustrate these themes.[22]

When I was a little girl, my family was on our way home from church one Sunday, and I was really upset because I felt Sunday school, which I was attending at the time, was a total disaster. I mean it was a total disaster—the boys were throwing spitballs, the kids were running around—it was a total lack of control and we weren't learning anything. So I announced to my parents that I wanted to stop going to Sunday school and instead go to the sanctuary to hear the sermon with the adults.

I suppose I thought that they'd think it was pretty good that I was so mature and that I wanted to hear the sermon rather than go to Sunday school. Instead, my Dad was furious, got very upset with me, and said, "Well, of course you'll keep going to Sunday school."

I protested and said, "But I'd get more out of the sermon."

And he said, "If you don't like Sunday school, then change it."

Well, I was probably twelve at the time and we attended a huge, downtown church in Minneapolis, and here was my father telling me to fix Sunday school. Well, yeah, sure Dad.

My Mom tried to rescue me and said, "Oh, Curt, that's unreasonable." But then he got mad at my Mother! The long and short of it is that my dad always got his way, and knowing I wasn't going to win, I started to cry.

That didn't do any good. When we got home, he sent me to my room, and I had to come downstairs later with a list of all the things that I thought were wrong with the Sunday school and all the ways I thought it could be fixed. He then reviewed the list with me and helped me refine it.

Then my mother had to get the number of the Sunday school superintendent, and I had to call him to make an appointment. Can't you imagine how I thought it would go? "Oh, hi, this is Marilyn Carlson, and you know, I'm in the sixth grade, and I have a few suggestions to fix Sunday school." As you can imagine, I thought it would go over really big.

In the end, the superintendent said, "Actually we've been worried about the Sunday school, and we would really appreciate your ideas."

So, sure enough, my mother, who always seemed to somehow get involved in the punishment for my sins, had to drive me downtown to the church in the middle of the week. We had a meeting, got other kids involved, and we fixed the Sunday school!

Carlson Companies was named one of the 100 Best Companies to Work for in America by Fortune in its February 4, 2002, edition.

MD. Carlson is chief medical officer and senior vice president for Clinical Affairs in the Cardiac Rhythm Management Division of St. Jude Medical, Inc. I had the privilege of working with him recently, and he recounted a personal story that showcases how 3D-Storytelling can inspire others to reconsider their purpose.[23]

Let me tell you today about how people, individuals, can make a difference whether they are dead or alive. And let's go back to 1969, if you will. Remember where you were that year? In 1969 a lot of journeys began, and that's where we'll begin this one as well. In 1969 Neil Armstrong and his friends journeyed to the moon. In 1969 the first Concord plane flew. The first 747 flew. A fellow by the name of Tom McClain launched a rowboat from the east coast of the United States and landed somewhere in Europe for the first time.

But all was not necessarily so good in 1969. About 450,000 Americans died suddenly that year. Just as they had in 1968. And every year for many years before that. Four hundred fifty thousand people. There were fewer than thirty American cities that had 450,000 people in 1969. Can you imagine an entire city disappearing over the course of a year? Sudden cardiac death was a major problem, but it was one that many of us took for granted—many of us other than a gentleman by the name of Michel Mirowski.

You see, in 1969 Michel Mirowski was a young physician whose most valued mentor had been not only a doctor, but a doctor with heart disease that ultimately led to sudden cardiac arrest. When Michel lost his mentor, he vowed that he would do everything he could to prevent sudden cardiac arrest from taking the lives of others' mentors or loved ones in the future. He began a journey to develop the implantable cardioverter defibrillator.

Where was I in 1969? I was fourteen years old, and I remember that year because I received my Eagle Scout award from perhaps my most valued mentor, Doug Paddock, my scoutmaster. He taught me many of the values that I hold dear to this very day: to be prepared, to do my duty to God and my country, and to obey the Scout Law. We'll come back to Doug Paddock later.

What happened in the next several years? Well, Michel Mirowski and his associates began to work on the implantable cardioverter defibrillator. They did all the basic research that needed to be done, and they worked with animals and did patient work. Eventually, the first implantable cardioverter defibrillator was implanted in a human being in the year 1980. Michel Mirowski in many ways had realized his dream. It hadn't been easy. I can remember him saying, "They laughed at me. They didn't think it could be done." He had a beautiful video of an implantable defibrillator that had been implanted in a dog. And when that dog experienced sudden cardiac death and fell to the ground, the implantable defibrillator fired and the dog woke up and stood up. When he first showed that video at a scientific conference, nobody believed him. They believed that the dog had been trained to lie down and go to sleep and then wake up.

Nobody believed what Michel Mirowski said, even after he had done it—that it could be done. They laughed at him. He couldn't even get his report published in a journal. But in 1980 it happened. That first defibrillator went in, and we know what's happened since. Thousands if not tens or hundreds of thousands of lives have been saved. But the other thing that happened in 1980 was that I graduated from medical school. I'd been encouraged to attend medical school by Doug Paddock, my scoutmaster. In fact, he wrote me a check for my first white lab coat. To this day that check sits on my desk next to a picture of him. But

Doug never saw me graduate. Before I graduated, he collapsed suddenly and died of sudden cardiac death. That implantable defibrillator hadn't come along quite early enough for Doug.

And what happened to me was that I saw very clearly what happens to families, to people, to a scout troop, to students, to young men, when they lose someone who's very important in their lives. I saw kids who didn't have the benefit of having Doug Paddock in their life, and I vowed on that day, before I ever knew anything about an implantable cardioverter defibrillator, that I would commit my life to preventing the horrors of sudden cardiac death. Well, the next several years, the next twenty years, I went through a traditional academic cardiology career. I treated many patients individually who had high risk for sudden cardiac death, some who had survived sudden cardiac death. I implanted defibrillators and I saw the benefits of those devices in many, many people. And I saw how those devices changed from being really very simple, very crude, the size of a brick with the intelligence of a brick, to devices that today are not much larger than a silver dollar and have the intelligence and the computing capacity of my laptop. I saw how these devices can do so much more for people than we ever dreamed that they would or that Michel Mirowski ever dreamed that they would.

And today, as the chief medical officer at St. Jude Medical, I'm no longer treating individual patients. In many respects, I'm treating thousands of patients, influencing their lives daily through the decisions we make, the clinical trials that we perform, and the wonderful devices that we're manufacturing today. And in many ways what we're facing in the future is much different than what we faced in 1980. In many respects, we can prevent sudden cardiac death. Now we need to better determine who can benefit from these devices. We need to get these devices to the 67 percent of patients who are at risk and will die suddenly but aren't currently indicated to receive a defibrillator.

The problems of today are different in other respects, too. These devices can, need to, and will provide daily benefit to our patients in the future. They need to be there not just when they're going to die but they need to be there every day to prevent that from ever occurring in the future. It's our challenge as a company to find ways that these devices can provide that daily benefit. It's our challenge to think not only of the populations of patients, but of the individual patients and the benefits that these devices can provide for them.

That's why on my desk at home is that picture of Doug Paddock. That picture of him in his scout uniform with his campaign hat on looking ever, ever so healthy just a couple of years before his untimely death. Doug looks me in the eye every morning and reminds me why it's important—why what I do is important and who I'm taking care of every day. Who are your Doug Paddocks?

Mining for Stories

The first thing a leader must get past is the disbelief that he or she has valuable stories to tell. I ask hundreds of leaders a year if they have any good stories, and many of them believe they do not have many or even any stories to tell. But the truth is far from this belief. Our lives are jam-packed with stories—we are all walking, breathing encyclopedias of experience. But just like we often must data-mine our company records for information, we must also mine our pasts for the stories they hold.

I believe there is a hierarchy in terms of story effectiveness. There are three levels of stories, and all levels can be effective. The top level is personal stories. Nothing trumps a leader's personal experience when that experience is being used through a story to improve or enhance a communication. The second level is stories about others we personally know. For example, when I tell stories about my long-time business partner and friend, Boyd, the stories are effective because of the personal relationship I had with Boyd. The third level is all other stories, including case studies, examples picked up from periodicals or blogs, and other sources. Notice how these three levels match the two primary methods of learning mentioned earlier—direct and indirect experience. I break the indirect "learning from others" into two parts to create levels two and three. Relating stories we have learned from others we know is more powerful, usually, than relating stories you have studied, heard about, or read about.

Have you ever worked for a boss who had three really great stories, but only three? You might even feel you are this boss. My advice is simple: you must have, at a minimum, twenty readily available, polished, rehearsed stories that you file away in your database for use at a moment's notice. This may sound like a lot, but it is not. Here is one simple method for mining stories that can help you uncover these first twenty in your repertoire. Take a spreadsheet type of arrangement and look for the best and worst stories across many different life categories.

Boss	Vacation	Customer Experience	Coworker	Project	Children	Etc.
Best						
Worst						

Work through this spreadsheet and you will easily find twenty stories. If you use 3D-Storytelling to practice them, by the time you finish twenty, you will be able to take any experience and easily use it to enhance your communication.

6

TUNE INTO EMOTIONS

N ear my home in Mason, Ohio, stands the WLW broadcasting tower. Regarded by some tower hunters as "radio engineer heaven,"[1] this Blaw-Knox-diamond-shaped structure was built by radio and television tycoon Powel Crosley Jr. during the golden age of radio broadcasting. Standing 831 feet and weighing 136 tons, this legendary tower has an amazing history. On May 2, 1934, president Franklin D. Roosevelt turned a gold key in the White House, unleashing the tower's five hundred thousand watts. The signal was so strong that WLW became known as the "Nation's Station."

A large pond was constructed next to the tower to supply the twelve hundred gallons of water per minute needed to cool the twenty one-hundred-thousand-watt tubes. The signal was so strong that nearby residents "heard voices" through their toasters, faucets, and dental work. Even today, at the FCC's maximum allowed fifty thousand watts, the powerful station can be heard from Detroit to Birmingham.

Emotions are the wattage of leadership communication. For this wattage to amount to something, you need a broadcast tower of authenticity so that these emotions can be heard. And as anyone in the AM broadcasting world (or the Internet blogging world) knows, if you don't tune in to the feelings of your constituents, they will not tune in to your station. Constituents constantly scan the emotional channel, tuning in to stations that inspire, encourage, and engage. Even engineers, economists, all members of the C-suite, scientists, and others who proclaim their lives are based solely upon the facts, tune in to information better when the emotional atmosphere is handled well, which is a huge component of emotional channel communication. Like it or not, the fictional Vulcanlike "highly rational equals highly controlled or totally suppressed emotions" mode of thinking simply doesn't work in real life. The emotional channel is as important to decision making, engagement, retention, and clear thinking as the factual or symbolic channels. And many a leader has earned some stripes through dealing with emotional channel issues.

"Scholars of interpersonal communication tell us that openness invites openness; disclosure, disclosure. Self-disclosure can accelerate our sense of intimacy in a relationship."[2] For some people, emotional distance equals safety. For others, emotional neutrality equals emotionally appropriate business attire. The research on leadership, and leadership communication in particular, reveals that both of these ideas are ineffectual. Staying safe is having emotions but no broadcast tower. Remaining neutral is a tower sending a weak signal. If the adage "don't let them see you sweat" is your default position, you may wind up not allowing constituents to see anything. The inability or unwillingness to understand or communicate your emotions and to let constituents know you understand and empathize with their feelings will result in a broadcast station with no listeners.

Our research shows the following fundamentals. As a leader, you must communicate your emotional state in socially appropriate ways that befit the culture and occasion if you want this channel to help you complete a vibrant movie. You must also communicate to your audience that you know how they are feeling about the subject of the message, even if you disagree with their emotional attitude. Having a lack of relevant empathy or incorrectly understanding the emotional states of your constituents creates emotional resistance to your message. And our research shows that this type of resistance is the most difficult to overcome. A pile driver of data is often inadequate to breach this resistance, whereas a modicum of empathy often can. To understand the emotional channel a bit more, it helps to know some of the basics as they apply to leadership communication.

Emotions 101

Emotional intelligence is the current moniker for the subject of how leaders and others deal with emotions. Eras gone by referred to it as "maturity." The substance of the topic is simple: it is the ability to perceive (sense and understand) your own emotions and the emotions of others, interpret the emotional signals in a relationship and understand what they mean, and manage your emotions and deal with others' emotional states. Simple to state. Not easy to do. Communicating on the emotional channel requires the same three things: (1) you have to communicate your emotions and accurately state others' emotional states, (2) explain what these states mean in context, and (3) influence either the maintenance of these states (keep inspiration and hope alive) or influence a change in emotional states (convert the cynics, rout apprehension, overturn feelings of failure).

"One of the many reasons why some people become leaders and others followers ... has ... a lot to do with ... the manner of a given individual [that] promote[s] certain emotional responses in others."[3] We follow leaders because of the feelings they inspire. We want our leaders to be inspiring so that our internal inspiration is ignited. In fact, that's how we know they are inspiring—if we become more energized, more galvanized, more passionate about our work. (It seems odd that in many companies we hire for passion but want all meetings, conversations, and public appearances to be emotionally neutral).

Popular myth may suggest that inspiring emotional cues from leaders are typically displayed using cheerleading or rock band stage tactics. John D. Mayer is a psychologist at the University of New Hampshire and a thought leader in the emotional intelligence arena. He suggests, "A person high in emotional intelligence may be realistic rather than optimistic and insecure rather than confident. Conversely, a person may be highly self-confident and optimistic but lack emotional intelligence. The danger lies in assuming that because a person is optimistic or confident, he or she is also emotionally intelligent, when, in fact, the presence of those traits will tell you nothing of the sort."[4]

Emotionally intelligent leaders have many different volumes and postures. They can be loud and energetic, or quiet and reserved. Regardless of style, when leaders are both emotionally intelligent and good communicators, they allow individuals to view their personal interiors and stoke others to greatness. They do this by communicating on the emotional channel.

As a reminder from our chapter on the brain, many business people like to believe that business is conducted on pure reasoning, devoid of messy emotions. We all know this is not true, even though we try very hard to believe that it is. When it comes to logic and emotional neural circuits, "There is no way to separate them."[5] And perhaps one of the reasons why emotional intelligence, in general, and emotional channel communication, specifically, are so important is that "The wiring of the brain at this point in our evolutionary history is such that connections from the emotional systems to the cognitive systems are stronger than connections from the cognitive systems to the emotional systems."[6]

Basic Emotions

Some people believe there is an infinite shading of emotional nuance. Novelists revel in their ability to create a mood depicting these various shades to bring the human condition to life. Simon Baron-Cohen is a professor of developmental psychopathology; a Fellow of Trinity College, Cambridge; and director of the Autism Research Center at the University of Cambridge. He has devoted his career to understanding mental development, specializing in the study of autism. He and his team decided to figure out exactly how many discrete emotional states exist. When asked by Steven Johnson what he found, Baron-Cohen laughed and said, "Four hundred and twelve."[7]

Now, that may or may not be the exact number, but one scientist at least has tried to find out. Knowing the exact number of emotions that exist may not be a leadership necessity, but understanding basic emotions can improve one's ability to perceive, understand, and convey information on the emotional channel. One of the most influential researchers to theorize about this basic emotional set is Robert Plutchik, professor emeritus of Yeshiva University's Albert Einstein College of Medicine in New York. His work suggests there are eight basic emotional states and that mixing these together creates a variety of other distinct emotional states. His idea works in a similar manner as the three primary colors that create the many hues and shades of color we labor over when repainting a kitchen. The eight basic emotions are anger, anticipation, joy, acceptance, fear, surprise, sadness, and disgust.

If you arranged these eight in the order listed above on something like a color wheel, by combining emotions that were adjacent to each other you could derive additional distinctive emotional states. For example, combine joy and acceptance and you get friendliness. Combine joy and surprise and you get alarm. If you look at the wheel and combine emotions that are not adjacent, you can derive other emotional states. Disgust and sadness yield remorse, while anticipation and fear yield anxiety.

Why is this concept important to leadership communication? It is important because the greater your range of emotional expression, the greater connection you will make with constituents. If you rely primarily on just declaring that you are filled with anticipation or are disgusted by recent events, these primary emotions may strongly indicate your emotional state (or the state of others), but a leader needs more emotional expressions to expertly convey the nuance and subtlety of occasions.

In *The Leadership Experience: From Individual Success to Organizational Significance,* a book I coauthored with Gregg Thompson, I detail a speech delivered by Václav Havel to the Czech Republic in 1991 while he was president.[8] At the time of the speech, things were quite gloomy, and Havel had a huge backload of emotional disappointment he needed to address from a logical, emotional, and symbolic viewpoint. Reading just the first half dozen paragraphs of his address reveals the following words that refer to or describe different emotional states:

bleak, astonished, surprise, anticipate, joyful, doubt, distress, pleasant, guilt, nervous, hope, fear, impatience, disappointment, malice, suspicion, shock, embarrassment, uncertainty

In just the first third of John F. Kennedy's inaugural address, he also refers to a variety of emotional states, often in a more stylized symbolic manner that was more appropriate for that period in history. Some of these emotional states are:

celebration, renewal, generosity, hardship, bitter, tempered, hope, foolish, misery, hostility, aggressive, temptation, weakness, sincerity, fear

It may be easy to argue that these political leadership examples were loaded with emotional phrases because the audiences were huge and political artistry requires emotional persuasion. But business leaders, too, such as those at TNT and LensCrafters, have also spoken in appropriate ways on the emotional channel. In fact, when business leaders are at their best, they are direct and unambiguous in declaring their emotional states to their constituents and in accurately portraying their general emotional mood.

Describing his transformation at LensCrafters, Dave Browne said, "I really felt like I was living two lives. At home and church I had love and respect in my life. At work it was only about numbers and winning. The day I realized I could bring these emotions from my personal life to work, my business relationships improved and so did our results."9

For the balance of his tenure as CEO, Browne couldn't go two sentences without using the words "head" and "heart" together. He described his change to using more emotional channel communication as the beginning of a "real romance." Speaking of LensCrafters' three-day, ten-year anniversary celebration, he said, "I cried, I laughed, I hugged and I danced. I put my tears and fears right out there." This addition of his emotional channel was a hard-fought and well-won battle for Browne and helped his executive team to understand the company's central movie in ways they had never been able to when he was strictly a numbers guy.

Deal with Emotions, or They Will Deal with You

Do strong emotional states influence decision making and gravely affect communication? Absolutely. Have you ever made a decision you later regretted when you were angry? Likely you have. Have you ever made a decision you later regretted when you were totally in love? Likely you have. During times of strong emotion we coach ourselves and others to take a walk around the block, gain some distance, wait a period of time (hold your breath and count to ten), or talk things over with others before making a decision. All of these are great ideas. Finding methods to sort through strong or mixed emotional states is a necessary component to managing your emotional intelligence. But sorting out your feelings is merely the first step.

Many leaders sort out their emotional states and then try to control them to the point of emotional calmness or neutrality. And indeed there are situations in which this is an appropriate countenance to assume. But maintaining this affect-free face mask is not the best way to communicate and influence on the emotional channel in all situations. A better methodology is to allow others, in appropriate ways, to understand your emotional state with regard to the subject of the communication. This requires leaders to show or directly state how they feel. You can describe feelings of pleasure, sadness, irritation, excitement, concern, doubt, hopefulness, and even passion without becoming overly wild in how these feelings are displayed. Not allowing those you lead to understand your emotional posture, especially when the issue is important, will only ignite their movie-making brain to try to guess and interpret your emotional state. And letting them fill in the blanks can result in their constructing movies that are simply not true about how you feel.

By the same token, you need to get in touch with and understand the emotional states of your constituents. "Taken as a whole, the message sent by neurological, psychological, and organizational research is startling in its clarity. Emotional leadership is the spark that ignites a company's performance, creating a bonfire of success or a landscape of ashes. Moods matter that much."[10]

The larger the group you lead, and the more geographically spread out they are from where you physically work, the more significant challenges you'll find in detecting mood, meaning basic emotional states. We typically know what mood others are in simply because of their proximity. We see others' faces, hear tones in their voices, hear folks talk about the general mood of the place, and employ other methods of staying tuned in to the group's mood. But when a leader's constituency is dispersed, these conduits of emotional information are at best constrained with a communication tourniquet and at worst cut. We simply have a far more difficult time gaining access to vital emotional information when we don't see and hear each other often.

For example, in their book *The Social Life of Information,* John Seely Brown and Paul Duguid showcase a typical scenario concerning Xerox's technical reps, who worked remotely from one another, and what they did when they got together for regular face-to-face meetings. "At these meetings, while eating, playing cribbage, and engaging in what might seem like idle gossip, the reps talked work, and talked continuously. The posed questions, raised problems, offered solutions, constructed answers, and discussed changes in their work, the machines, or customer relations. In this way, both directly and indirectly, they kept one another up to date with what they knew, what they learned, and what they did."[11]

No news flash. We've all experienced these get-togethers. One way of classifying these meetings, which is what Brown and Duguid suggest, is a huge social exchange of information, because humans are wired for such exchanges. And in every one of these meetings the emotional channel component worked far more easily than it would in any online exchange, because people had more direct access to emotional channel information, portrayed through tone and gesture. What's surprising to learn is that those who are better at communicating their emotional states use nonverbal visual cues in a more effective manner than others and can affect the mood of the group more. This means such people are likely the better regulators of both information and mood than others.

Researchers have known for a long time that nonverbal cues really play a huge role in conveying emotional signals. People who are more nonverbally expressive are seen as better communicators and are more likable. Those who display a larger range of expressions are viewed as more self-confident and garner larger social networks than others. It even goes further. Some researchers put three strangers in a room together and asked them not to speak. Those with the greater range of nonverbal cues, even without trying or being asked to try, were able to transmit their mood to the other two far more successfully.[12]

You can't deal with your emotions or the emotions of your constituents as well through a Blackberry as you can in person. Out of necessity you may need to use a wide variety of technology to communicate with those you simply cannot see face-to-face often, but if all you ever communicate is facts, figures, numbers, and other technical information, your leadership communication effectiveness (and your overall leadership effectiveness) will be less than what you could achieve otherwise.

Verbal and Nonverbal Emotional Communication

It would be easy to continue to cite evidence that mood matters, that emotional issues are difficult to deal with, and that emotional intelligence as manifested through communication distinguishes good leaders from the best leaders. You can choose to believe it or not, but the research about these matters is clear. The question Boyd and I wrestled with is how to communicate better on the emotional channel.

We've already suggested some ideas: get as clear as you can about your own feelings, or be prepared to communicate your mixed feelings about the matter at hand. Find numerous methods for staying in touch with the mood, feelings, and emotional states of your constituents. This likely means more phone calls (this allows for vocal tonality input, and the immediacy of a phone call can invite more honest emotional responses than even instant messaging), more face-to-face meetings (real or virtual through video), and more rigor in asking others how they feel about the business. Today's business pace pressures many leaders to act and to order without understanding what movie is playing. Some of the best leaders we studied spent time on a daily basis checking in on how things were going emotionally with their disparate constituencies, just as they checked in on what actions had taken place.

Since we live in a more virtual workplace today, the burden for declaring our emotional states has increased. When leaders and constituents are in the same room, everyone can pick up the mood. This proximity helps but can still be insufficient when communicating on the emotional channel. The following three ideas will help you communicate better on the emotional channel.

1. **Clarify Your Feelings.** Get clear about your emotions, and expand your ability to describe them well. This can take some work, but sorting your feelings and working through the mixed feelings that most leadership issues stimulate is the first step.

2. **Gather Emotional Information.** Talk to your constituents more often about how they feel. When you hear a tone of dissatisfaction, interest, excitement, or other mood, try to find out why they might be having these feelings. If you cannot speak very directly to some individuals because of relationship irritations or estrangements, speak with colleagues who might be able to confide information that helps you gain insight. We're not talking about staffing "emotional police" in every office or trying to use indirect means of finding out what's up for bad reasons. We are suggesting using some basic social intelligence to keep up with how attitudes and moods are changing and what is causing the shifts.

3. **Plan Your Emotional Communication.** Having worked at figuring out how you feel and how your constituency feels allows you to plan for how you will address the emotional channel. Be sure

you let your constituents know that you do know how they feel, even if there are a variety of emotional states among them. The worst thing you can do is gloss over these states, or even worse, ignore them.

We began this chapter with the radio tower metaphor. We leave you with this thought: **Are your constituents tuning you in or tuning you out?** The answer to this question largely depends on how well you gather emotional intelligence and on your ability to communicate about emotional states. We follow leaders because of the feelings they stimulate in us. Yet the very process of becoming a leader creates emotional distance. Don Clarke encountered this dilemma at age thirty-eight. He was one of the youngest people ever to be promoted to CEO and chairman of a major division at the multi-billion dollar May Company before it merged with Macy's. The day before taking the job full-time, the retiring CEO and chairman congratulated Clarke and paraphrased a statement he'd once heard, saying, "Tomorrow two things will be true that are not true today. First, you will be CEO. Second, you have heard the truth for the last time."

Constituents rarely provide negative feedback to executives about their communication directly. When leaders give a bad face-to-face speech, the public feedback is positive, sometimes glowing. A lack of truthful feedback widens emotional distance and erodes trust, which creates even more communication barriers. This fear of telling the truth reinforces the leader's impression that his or her communication was powerful and clear. And even when leaders do receive anonymous, indirect feedback from organizational surveys, or read anonymous blogs that lampoon their actions, they lack the specificity, immediacy, and directness of having a constituent simply telling them frankly how he or she feels in the moment.

Leaders often feel a lack of feedback, or the insensitivity of bludgeoning blogarazzi lets them off the hook. The unfortunate truth is that frustrated leaders, relieved by either positive feedback or annoyed by the difficulties of indirect feedback, would rather accept the praise or discount the noise than seek the truth. Without absolving constituents, we suggest that fixing the problem is still primarily your own responsibility.

7

THE ALTAR OF DATA

People love facts. We gobble and regurgitate sports statistics, weather data, calorie counts, business indicators, and gas prices. Factoid junkies play parlor trivia games. Investors breathlessly track the rise and fall of a selection of their favorite market indicators on a minute-by-minute basis, updating their favorite mental model of how the stock market works. We are media-bludgeoned by the latest facts on crime, trade imbalances, pollen counts, death tolls, hair loss, and box office records. Some people will never know who won last night's game, while others know individual players' middle names, scoring average, lifetime league ranking, and high school mascot. Even though people track different facts or track facts differently, the reality is, we are all tuned to the factual channel.

Attention to quality has changed how business attends to data. We have proven that data-based decision making improves the quality of products and processes while often reducing the cost of both. A generation of business workers has learned the importance of measuring things well and the usefulness of stockpiling data. We hoard data like depression-era sufferers hoarded food. Data warehousing and data mining are essential business means, but these means do not define the ends. In our new data-rich world we find ourselves working like Bob Cratchit recording inputs and Ebenezer Scrooge counting outputs. All the while missing the meaning of our data and our work.

Russian physiologist, psychologist, and Nobel laureate Ivan Pavlov spent a lifetime pursuing science with an eye toward intellectual rigor. He first made important discoveries about the digestive system, which led him to conditioned reflex and the salivating dogs that were forever attached to his name. But in all of his efforts he pursued the ideal of obtaining scientific truth through empirical study. He constantly reminded his students to remember the purpose of facts: "Don't become a mere recorder of facts, but try to penetrate the mystery of their origin."[1]

Factual types of information include data, measures, numbers, trends, evidence, opinions, reasoned judgments, assertions, numerical analysis, and even a moistened index finger to the wind. Facts teach, persuade, and entertain. They can be distorted, misrepresented, and illogically used to support dubious conclusions. Business leaders often communicate only facts and presume that others will share their interpretation. PLEASE presume they will not. Facts do not speak for themselves, despite the common adage that they do. The factual channel is an extraordinarily important channel, but it is only one of three through which we construct our sense and meaning of the world.

Factual Truth

There are numerous (notice how the word "numerous" suggests a relatively big number without being specific) books about the use of numbers and how the same fact can be interpreted in many different ways. Many authors use interesting, dramatic, amusing, and emphatic stories to illustrate their points on raw facts, distorted statistics, and unreliable data.

A number of good books have been written on the subject of facts, one of which is Joel Best's *Damned Lies and Statistics: Untangling Numbers from the Media, Politicians, and Activists.*[2] Best showcases many examples of how numbers are so poorly quoted that even the average interpreter of the facts can see through the problem. In one case he refers to a PhD candidate who reported that the number of children gunned down in America has doubled since 1950. I have shown this statement to hundreds of managers, most of who easily and readily remark, "This can't be true. If you double every year from 1950, the number becomes astronomically large." And of course they are correct. Start with just one child losing his life to a gunshot in 1950 and then double this number. By the time you arrive at 1980 (roughly when Generation Y, or the Millennial, or iGen generation started), the number of children losing their lives in gun-related deaths is more than one billion (1,073,741,824, which is 2^{30}, or thirty years of doubling).

John Allen Paulos is a well-known mathematician whose concerns largely revolve around innumeracy. He argues, persuasively, that the average person (including the average manager) uses basic mathematical or logical reasoning poorly due to poor education or to the rigor that mathematical reasoning requires. Paulos has written numerous books and articles, and his *A Mathematician Reads the Newspaper* is on the readers' list of the Random House Modern Library's compilation of the one hundred best nonfiction books of the century.[3] In this book he provides the following straightforward example.

> Imagine buying 100 pounds of potatoes and being told that they're 99 percent water. After the potatoes have been left outdoors for a day or two, you're told that they're now 98 percent water. At first, it doesn't seem difficult to determine the weight of the slightly dehydrated potatoes, but I've discovered that few people can do so.[4]

We know some of you are wondering where the trick in this math problem lies, some of you instantly see the answer, and some of you really don't like this kind of math problem (we will reveal the answer later on). This difference among people is what is important about the illustration, not the answer per se. Some of us get math and see logical relationships. Some of us always question data and its credibility regardless of its source. And some of us simply would rather not be bothered by having to do the math in our heads or on paper or with a computer, because what we want at the end of the day is an answer, not the complexity of deriving the answer. These are the problems leaders face every day. Some people get the data easily, others don't believe the data no matter what, and some want the conclusion without the stress of knowing how the conclusion was derived.

Chip and Dan Heath, in their book *Made to Stick: Why Some Ideas Survive and Others Die* (which is organized, curiously, around the ideas of facts, credibility, emotionality, and stories—another confirmation of **this** book's thesis), use a wide variety of examples about how to make your data come alive. Their ideas about concreteness, surprise, emotional relevance, and the use of stories as methods to make information, ideas, policies, and modes of thought stick in the minds of people are well considered and wonderfully interesting.[5]

And as a final example of the numerous (there's that word "number" again) books that one can read for information or entertainment or both is *UnSpun: Finding Facts in a World of Disinformation,* by Brooks Jackson and Kathleen Hall-Jamieson. One of the key objectives of this book is to "Explain how to recognize spin, how to understand its nature, and how to spot the techniques spinners use to deceive." The authors use a variety of wonderful commercial and political examples to state their case that "Not only are we surrounded by commercial and political pitchmen who are trying their best to pull the wool over our eyes, but also our own brains betray us in ways that psychologists are struggling to understand."[6]

Facts Well Represented

Leaders rely on facts to make decisions. They also want constituents to understand the facts so that they will contribute their intelligence to the decision-making process. Part of this process is exploring and organizing all the available facts. The critical moment comes when facts must be communicated either from the bottom up or the top down.

Unfortunately, it's often the communication that fails rather than the facts. Yes, facts can obscure the truth, be twisted, and lead to multiple interpretations, but it's the communication that often is the perpetrator of poor movies.

There is an entire industry devoted to understanding facts and communicating them. Feasibility consultants look at all the facts ...... and even the kitchen sink. Whether it's looking at a new mixed-use development or a new restaurant, they study population, average household size, income, families, median age, racial characteristics, competing businesses, and all the financial numbers, such as per capita costs. And the list goes on and on.

As you can imagine, making sense of all of these facts and communicating them clearly and concisely is quite a challenge. The founding father of the feasibility industry is Harrison "Buzz" Price. The eighty-something's book, *Walt's Revolution! By the Numbers,* is a wonderful read.[7] For the last couple of decades he has run the Harrison Price Company. Before that he founded Economics Research Consultants. He got his start at Stanford Research in the 1950s. It was there that one of his professors first taught him about communicating facts. "He taught us how to create great graphics that could jump out of your head."

Buzz is a numbers guy, and when our colleague Geoff Thatcher spoke to him as we researched stories about the effective use of facts in communication, Geoff saw how Buzz made numbers come alive. When Buzz talks about numbers, metaphors roll off his tongue. He describes them as musical notes, a living language, points on an economic map, and signals. To him, understanding numbers is like economic geography. Communicating the facts is like taking people on a journey. The secret, according to Buzz, is to use numbers to tell a great story. "The x and y axis are great tuners of communication."

Buzz even communicates with great emotion about numbers. "They make me wake up in the middle of the night and say 'OH!' Even when I don't have to pee." Actually, Buzz says "emotion" is the wrong word. "You have to be passionate about your numbers. You have to be in the right spirit of it." We talked to some of his colleagues, and this is what they had to say about his communication skills:

"He's got the Technicolor to go with the numbers."

"He shoots arrows as straight as they can go."

"A tremendous number of other feasibility people love to obfuscate what they do. Buzz goes right to the heart of it."

"He's an outstanding communicator. Very precise and concise."

Buzz is a legend for a variety of reasons. He has conducted or managed more than six thousand feasibility studies. He's been roasted, toasted, and inducted more times than he'd like to remember. However, Buzz is probably most famous for his first client. In 1955 he got a phone call from a "movie guy." A few weeks later he was standing in an Anaheim orange grove. Buzz was paid twenty-five thousand dollars and given eight weeks to find a location for the new Disneyland theme park. From the start, he said, three potential locations were identified—the San Fernando Valley, the Pomona<N>San Gabriel area, and somewhere along the planned I-5 corridor. Buzz evaluated a host of dimensions. Among other things, he took temperatures and analyzed smog levels and growth patterns. At the end of the evaluation process, he prepared a report for Walt Disney.

As Geoff peppered Buzz with questions, trying to get him to remember speaking and interacting with Walt Disney, Buzz spoke in the same language he always does. In other words, the same principles that would work for a small developer in the Midwest worked for Walt. "I cut through the chaos of numbers and cut right to the chase." In this case, it was to communicate that Anaheim was the best place for Walt to build Disneyland.

Buzz worked for years with Walt, but he never joined the Disney Company. Both knew it was best for the "strategic planner" to be outside. It insulated Buzz from the management structure at Disney. As he told Walt then, "You won't listen to me if I'm on the payroll."

While Walt Disney's great successes are well chronicled, some of this creative genius's ideas were shelved because the numbers didn't support them. Some of the 110 studies Buzz conducted were, in his own words, "negative." There was the attraction at Niagara Falls and an indoor park in St. Louis. Buzz also looked at locations near Washington, D.C., and Palm Beach, Florida, for what eventually came to be Disney World, in Orlando, Florida.[8]

There is a naïve business fallacy suggesting that statistics establish facts. However, we believe leaders understand that the reverse is true. Leaders assert a goal, vision, and/or agenda and then test for statistical likelihood. They allow facts to inform their interpretation so that they can improve decision making and communication.

Logic

Our research indicates that constituents have two important concerns when listening to leaders communicate the facts—beyond the obvious need to believe that the leader's numbers are credible and that he or she is not engaging in some fraudulent data doping or sloppy data mismanagement. The first concern is that the leader's facts add up; that they make sense; that evidence, regardless of how tight or loose its empirical nature, is logical. And the second concern is that the leader showcases the facts in a manner that allows constituents to follow their logic.

Not all facts are data in the sense of measurements, calculations, or analyses. Some facts are simple assertions. We assert that customers are our only focus, that we are the best company to work for, and that our products and services are the best, even when proving any of these statements exactly and precisely might be a bit tricky. Other assertions that help us see the logic in a train of thought have to do with past decisions. For example, we refer to how we took the right-hand path in the fork of the road two years ago, not to reopen the data analysis of that decision, but simply to remind people of historic events that provide a reason to understand the current information. Some facts are simply raw data. Others are derived data from analysis. Some facts compete with one another for the truth. At the end of the day, leaders must assemble raw data, derived data, assertions, and other forms of "logic" and assemble them into logical stories that help guide their constituents' thinking and facilitate their understanding of the logic behind our decisions. At the end of the day, most decisions made by leaders are based upon conflicting sets of information, insufficient or questionable data input, and plenty of critics who believe that their factual information is superior and "correct."

Facts May Not Be Boring, But You Might Be

Communicating facts well is far more difficult than regurgitating data. It requires the same skill as good storytelling. Numbers are the language of business. Unfortunately, this language can be dull and tedious when spoken by most leaders. Reading data aloud to groups, especially in monotone, is B-O-O-O-R-I-N-G. Displaying stacks of facts during a presentation or in writing can put audiences to sleep. Constituents soon tune out because they can read faster than you can speak or write your thoughts. Worse, they may conclude that you have not analyzed the data.

The leader's communication job is more interpretation than recitation. Minimal data presentation and maximum interpretation usually converts boring to interesting. Stand ready to share the larger collection of facts that influenced your decision, but showcase your thinking, not the data for data's sake. This applies to written communication, too.

Make Facts Memorable

Simple and approximate visual analogies can make data understandable and memorable. For example, an acre is about the size of an American football field, goal line to goal line (48,000 square feet versus an acre, which is 43,560 square feet). Not a bad, quick visual comparison. In an article for *Stanford Business*, Kathleen O'Toole quotes professor Chip Heath, a Stanford-trained psychologist, on the subject:

"People do care about the truth of an idea, but they also want to tell stories that produce strong emotion, and that second tendency sometimes gets in the way of the first.

"If we could understand what kinds of stories succeed beyond all expectations, even when they are not true, we might be able to take legitimate information, about health for example, and change people's behavior for the better," Heath says. "Or if I were a business manager, I would love to have a mission statement for my organization that was as successful at moving through the organization as the most successful urban legends."

Much evidence suggests that people are very poor at remembering facts such as statistics, while they are better at remembering and repeating ideas cast as narratives or as analogies. "This is hard for our MBA students to accept, because I think business people in general think that facts speak for themselves," Heath says.[9]

Fact: From 1960 to 2000 the number of iron ore mines in northern Minnesota was reduced from 284 to 7 while the number of mine employees went from 48,000 to 6,700. To make these data more memorable, Thomas Peluso, vice president and general manager of National Steel Company's Pellet Plant in Keewatin, Minnesota, framed this information with his personal history. He had worked his way up from an overall-wearing miner to a tie-wearing executive. He told us:

Most of the iron ore in the United States comes from the Mesabi Mountain range north of Duluth. Glaciers ground an old ridge to form these gentle rolling mounds of free iron ore. In 1960 we had 284 mines and approximately 48,000 mine employees up there, pounding the mountain into rubble. By 2000 there were only 7 mines and 6,700 employees. Yet, we mined about 50 million tons of ore every year for forty years. We started with lots of people and small machines, and now we do it with fewer people and monster machines.[10]

Visual imagery like Peluso uses can provide memorable context. Using physical pictures or word pictures is a time-honored method of helping facts stick. In 1921 the national advertising manager for the Street Railways Advertising Company, Frederick R. Barnard, composed the phrase, "One look is worth a thousand words."[11] He later modified this to "ten thousand words." The adage "A picture is worth a thousand words" is the common adaptation of his original phrase. And according to courtroom guru and attorney Lou Giligan, "The right picture is worth a hundred thousand dollars in the courtroom."[12]

Visual Display of Data

We agree with Edward Tufte, who asserts that graphics are not "devices for showing the obvious to the ignorant."[13] While a variety of software has granted permission to the graphical Michelangelo that lives in every business person, distorting data unintentionally because this impish internal artist insists on color, depth, and impact only makes you appear to be an amateur. It is nearly impossible to communicate business ideas and issues without supporting charts, tables, or graphs. Visually expressing the meaning (perhaps the poetry) of numbers is a daunting task, whether written or during oral presentation.

Graphical displays either share data or aid you as you persuade others to accept your point of view. The facts should be accurate, clear, and support the interpretation. The title of the chart should state the point you are making. The chart itself should be simple enough to be understood by the average high school student. Learn to display data accurately and in ways that support information and meaning. Once you have mastered the basics, then you can proceed to higher levels of mastery, which usually encompass a more artistic view of how to display facts and get people to discuss the logic of ideas by deepening the focus of the issue.

Here's an example of how to use visual aids to combine several different channels of information to create a "logical debate" over the future course of a company. And a computer and projector were not necessary to achieve the intended effect. For a time while Don Pierce was president of Arby's Inc., Boyd was helping the senior team sort through a series of tough decisions about the fast-food company's stores, both corporate and franchise. The franchise owners were loyalists to the brand. Boyd often told me that if you "cut an Arby's franchise owner, they would bleed Arby's sauce."

While working with the company before an annual franchisers' meeting, a senior executive privately expressed to Boyd his concerns about Don's speaking ability. "Don is a great leader and a great communicator, but his last speech, his last couple of presentations were, uh, well—boring. Could you work with him?"

It stunned Boyd to hear this. Don is a great strategist, a charming person, and Boyd never considered him boring. But listening to the executive's concern, Boyd decided to approach Don and during one of his coaching meetings said, "Don, the word on the street is that your last speech was pretty boring."

"Oh, it's worse than that. I've been working on public speaking for ten years just to get this bad," Don laughed. His candor opened the door for some rapid examination of the root causes as to why his communication was experienced as boring. First of all, others often wrote his speeches, and when Don resorted to reading them aloud, he came across as a typical, monotonic, facts-only-oriented CEO. His genuineness and authenticity were lost during these recitals. Many of the franchisers recognized Don's analytic brilliance but were resisting his progressive ideas because of the nature of these lackluster communications.

Don needed to find a way that could reveal his credibility and bring his data alive to spark the discussion that would allow franchisers the opportunity to go beyond the numbers themselves and get to the meaning of those numbers. Don and Boyd worked feverishly for a couple of days and decided to depart from all earlier methods. First, Don would not speak from notes. He knew his numbers. Second, he would spend the first hour in the meeting speaking about what he cared for the most—his strategic vision. Third, he would just be himself, the guy everyone actually liked and respected, and stop trying to assume some fictional image of a corporate CEO.

And last, Don and Boyd decided on how to display the facts in a more stimulating and interesting manner. The meeting room was lined with poster-size images of Arby's history, a real photo journal of the progress the company had made over time. The room was set up so that a central table occupied the visual field of all in attendance. This table was covered during Don's first hour of heart-to-heart communication about the facts, vision, and power of a company to do what it set its mind to. At the end of the prelude, Don approached the covered table and with a flourish unveiled twenty-one bottles of beer. The franchisers chuckled, and because they had been warmed by Don's frankness in the beginning, were readily engaged in where he was going with his beer demonstration.

"Who is the Budweiser of the QSR [quick-service restaurant] industry?" Don asked, holding the Budweiser bottle aloft.

"McDonald's," someone shouted, which got a ripple of laughter. Picking up a Coors bottle, Don looked at it in his hand for a moment and then held it up to the audience and asked, "Burger King?"

Another round of laughter, and at this point everyone was getting what he was driving at. When he held up the Michelob bottle, he didn't even have to say anything, as several in the audience shouted, "Wendy's!"

Allowing the laughter to subside, Don shifted his posture and looked at the remaining bottles. After a short pause, he swept his hand across the remaining eighteen bottles and asked in a more serious and sober tone, "And who are we?"

After a moment of silence, the crowd erupted in conversation. Everyone wanted to talk about who they were, what they represented, and how the vision Don had spoken of applied to his metaphor. They voiced their dreams: "We want to be Samuel Adams!" And they disclosed their worst fears: "Have we become Old Milwaukee?" Allowing the discussion to roll for a while, Don regained their attention and continued.

He spoke to the group about how the facts were forcing them to consider a new direction for the sake of retaining their devotion to a brand they had staked their livelihoods on. He shared his dream of brand development and dual branding with other QSR franchises. While some still struggled with the message even though they got the "logic," others came around. At the end of his speech, the senior executive who had first approached Boyd with his concerns about Don's boring communication style rushed up and exclaimed, "Man, why didn't we video this? The whole company needs to see this!"[14]

And we would agree with this statement. The whole company needs to see the logic of the facts, not just the streams of charts and graphs that display the data. Facts alone seldom persuade and rarely inspire insight, perspective, or sound decision making.

Amazing Facts

Using amazing facts can alter viewpoints in an instant. Amazing facts are the diamonds of information found in mountains of data. They can at once convey facts, emotion, and symbols as they lead a person's mind to rapidly fill in the blanks. Try some of these on for size.

There are 76 rivers in the world that are 1,000 miles long or longer. And 22 of them flow through Russia.[15]

The Burj Dubai in Dubai, UAE, is planned to be an 818-meter-tall (2,684-foot-tall) skyscraper with 156 completed floors. Projected for a 2009 completion, this will be the tallest man-made structure of any kind in history.[16]

The longest movie in the world is The Cure For Insomnia, which runs over 87 hours and would need 18 DVD's to show it—that is, if it is ever put on DVD.[17]

A buzzard can spot a rodent from nearly three miles away.[18]

The answer to the potato question at the beginning of this chapter is 50 pounds. Since 99 percent of the original 100 pounds of potatoes is water, only one pound is not water. This pound does not dehydrate, and so after a day or two it represents 2 percent of the total of partially dehydrated potatoes remaining, which means the total weight equals 50 pounds.[19]

The natural fascination humans have for amazing facts, solving puzzles (like the potato question), and other types of novelty is well known. And amazing facts can be very useful as a device to help the factual channel's logic become clearer and more memorable. There is a danger, however, in that some amazing facts are distortions of the truth that nevertheless have a ring of truth in them, or that become true despite their illogical basis. These facts become what Joel Best calls "mutant statistics."[20] These are the kinds of amazing statistics or factual statements that have been exaggerated to the point of being false, but have been represented so many times by so many authorities in so many ways that we accept them without critical thought. Call them urban legends if you like. The difficulty for the leader is to avoid creating these factual errors and to disprove those that already exist.

Logical Reasoning

Plenty of experts have devoted time and energy to concerns about reasoning fallacies, so we are choosing not to cover the subject in detail here. Obtaining, massaging, and then displaying the facts can still be guided by one of several illogical processes, such as "jumping to conclusions." An example of this for a Web design company might be "Web traffic has increased by 20 percent at our competitors, and ours has decreased by 5 percent. They must have a better look than we do." But loads of other reasons could explain these facts.

Jumping to too many conclusions can lead to "fuzzy generalizations." Stereotypical thinking is like "couch potato reasoning"—letting your brain rely upon certain "well-known truths" to guide your judgment rather than asking a couple of informed questions and upgrading your ability to make better decisions. To continue the Web design illustration: "Our competitors always beat us at Web design.

It's because they have those Silicon Valley brains and coastal-born-and-bred chic designers, and we're stuck with Midwestern talent. You know, solid, corn-fed designers. Nice but uninteresting."

Another illogical mode of reasoning accompanies a lot of power-prone leaders. Call it the "prove me wrong" fallacy. Simply assert something is true and shift the burden of proof to the opponent. "We have the best designers east of the Mississippi. How are you gonna dispute that?"

And of course there is the garden variety of "graphic lies," as well as displays that are cleverly designed to mislead. Garden-variety graphic lies can be unintentional and usually arise from the inexpert use of charts and graphs. But sometimes visual aids are deliberately designed to misguide judgment by distorting data in a particular manner. Whether inexpert or malicious, graphic lies are exactly that—lies.

Organizing Facts

Many leaders work hard at data collection and analysis. They also sort through the less empirical factual evidence of opinion, values, and intentions to derive decisions about everything from where and how to hold a meeting to strategic direction. Leaders can invest a great deal of time in thinking about how to organize their logical thoughts and present them to a group. Other times they just wing it; sometimes this works and sometimes it doesn't. Great logic can be disguised, distorted, or diminished without considering how to arrange the facts so that others can follow the logic. There are a variety of methods for organizing the flow of your logical discourse. You may want to consider the following as templates you can use.

Past/Present/Future

This is a classic timeline form of organizing an argument. Many different time series displays can be used as aids to this organizing principle. Just be careful that past conclusions are reconsidered in the light of present circumstances. As we will discuss further in the last chapter, this form of presenting information is especially important when you are communicating about future states, updating your central movie, or discussing strategy.

Pro/Con

Most of us have conducted this type of analysis when weighing important considerations. It can be an effective way to communicate a decision, especially when a dilemma has been presented. A historic example of this kind of reasoning can be found in a letter from Benjamin Franklin to Joseph Priestly (a contemporary of Franklin's who was both a pastor and an inventor, and is credited with discovering the process for making soda water):

London, September 19, 1772

Dear Sir,

In the Affair of so much Importance to you, wherein you ask my Advice, I cannot for want of sufficient Premises, advise you what to determine, but if you please I will tell you how.

When these difficult Cases occur, they are difficult chiefly because while we have them under Consideration all the Reasons pro and con are not present to the Mind at the same time; but sometimes one Set present themselves, and at other times another, the first being out of Sight. Hence the various Purposes or Inclinations that alternately prevail, and the Uncertainty that perplexes us.

To get over this, my Way is, to divide half a Sheet of Paper by a Line into two Columns, writing over the one Pro, and over the other Con. Then during three or four Days Consideration I put down under the different Heads short Hints of the different Motives that at different Times occur to me for or against the Measure. When I have thus got them all together in one View, I endeavour to estimate their respective Weights; and where I find two, one on each side, that seem equal, I strike them both out:

If I find a Reason pro equal to some two Reasons con, I strike out the three. If I judge some two Reasons con equal to some three Reasons pro, I strike out the five; and thus proceeding I find at length where the Ballance lies; and if after a Day or two of farther Consideration nothing new that is of Importance occurs on either side, I come to a Determination accordingly.

And tho' the Weight of Reasons cannot be taken with the Precision of Algebraic Quantities, yet when each is thus considered separately and comparatively, and the whole lies before me, I think I can judge better, and am less likely to take a rash Step; and in fact I have found great Advantage from this kind of Equation, in what may be called Moral or Prudential Algebra.

Wishing sincerely that you may determine for the best, I am ever, my dear Friend,

Yours most affectionately

B. Franklin[21]

Cause/Effect

This is the brass ring of reasoning. Many business decisions are based upon trend analysis, correlated data, and circumstantial evidence, because finding true cause-and-effect relationship is empirically difficult to calculate. Use this method with caution. Or if you intend to use it in a loose manner, let your audience know that you are reasoning from cause/effect based upon some assumptions that may or may not be as provable as you would like. Just because a cause/effect rationale cannot be nailed down to the fifth decimal doesn't mean this form of connecting-the-dots reasoning is necessarily bad.

Break-Even

This is a much-used method of helping constituents see where an important tipping point or change might occur, as well as the accompanying shift in behavior required to capitalize on the opportunity.

Lesser of Two Evils

This is a particularly good organizing principle when a difficult decision must be reached regarding loss. This type of organizing principle is often used during situations such as downsizing, reallocating resources, restructuring facilities, or mergers.

Right vs. Wrong and Right vs. Right

These two forms of reasoning are used primarily when moral or ethical issues are at stake. Determining if a decision is morally correct or not (right versus wrong) can be easy or enormously difficult. Displaying the various steps of consideration concerning a right vs. wrong decision can help guide others through the reasoning process used to derive an answer. Right vs. right decision making is often even more difficult, because a leader is attempting to choose between two positively held values. Perhaps the most common example of this is choosing between the financial and social responsibilities an organization bears.

Dissuasion

This is the classic method of arguing from an opposite point of view. It is a way of pointing at what you want by communicating what you do not want. Leo Burnett, the famed marketing and advertising genius of the highly regarded Leo Burnett agency used this organizing principle for his valedictory address when he retired. Delivered on December 1, 1967, it was titled "When to Take My Name Off the Door." The entire speech is worth a read, but below are excerpts that showcase this form of reasoning from the opposite.

> But let me tell you when I might demand that you take my name off the door. That will be the day when you spend more time trying to make money and less time making advertising—our kind of advertising.
>
> When you forget that the sheer fun of ad-making and the lift you get out of it—the creative climate of the place—should be as

important as money to the very special breed of writers and artists and business professionals who compose this company of ours and make it tick. When you lose that restless feeling that nothing you do is ever quite good enough.

When you lose your itch to do the job well for its own sake—regardless of the client, or the money or the effort it takes ...... When you stop reaching for the manner, the overtone, the marriage of words and pictures that produces the fresh, the memorable and the believable effect ...

Finally, when you lose your respect for the lonely man—the man at his typewriter or his drawing board or behind his camera or just scribbling notes with one of our big black pencils—or working all night on a media plan. When you forget that the lonely man—and thank God for him—has made the agency we now have possible. When you forget he's the man who, because he is reaching harder, sometimes actually gets hold of—for a moment—one of those hot, unreachable stars.[22]

Classic W

This is the storytelling method that is most commonly taught in creative writing classes. The shape of the letter "W" describes how it works. Starting at the upper left of the "W" is where most stories begin. The stage is set, and the main characters and background are established. Then the story takes a dive downward (first downward stroke of the letter). A problem arises, a crisis forms, or a series of challenges are formulated (evil comes to town). The business or individual rebounds from these, and it appears victory is in sight (middle of the "W"). But then another, perhaps even graver, problem arises, and the company or individual is plunged back down (evil has more tricks up its sleeve). However, in the end the business or individual succeeds. An interesting number of case studies follow this general form.

Journalistic

This one is simple and straightforward. This organizing idea answers the questions who, what, when, where, why, and how.

Finding and using facts is not as easy as it seems at times, but neither is it as difficult as it looks. There are times when factual analysis is the content and context of a problem-solving discussion, and in these cases the factual channel can dominate the movie making. But when the analysis is finished, the cases weighed and evaluated, and decisions derived, the leader's job is to help constituents see the logic of the facts, and how a leader organizes this logic can be the difference between constituents buying in to or rejecting the movie.

8

LOSING YOUR VOICE

W e've already made the case for what can cause your voice to lose impact, even if you have mastered the three channels and are known for your superior communication skills. There are three other dimensions (call them competencies if you'd like) that when compromised will cause your voice to weaken, lose impact, and even have effects that are not what you intended. These three dimensions are credibility, vision, and connection. Lose the ability to be trusted, and your voice is discounted to below-Wal-Mart prices. Keep people lost in the fog long enough, and they will discount your communication and leadership to the point of derision. Invest sparingly or negatively in the emotional and social connection with the very people or process you are leading, and constituents will vote you out of office, even if they still engage in the masquerade of appearing to obey your commands.

The passages that follow shed a little light on these three leadership domains. Credibility is likely a universal condition for communication believability for any individual, leading or not. But if you choose to lead, then all three of these domains are critical to your leadership communication.

Credibility: Earning the Right to Be Heard

Iain Morris was a middle manager with Motorola's Paging Products Group when we first encountered his leadership ability. Several years ago the company had invited us to work with his engineering group that was responsible for new designs. At the time, the marketplace was exploding with demand for new pagers. They were immersed in the new-product-cycle pressure cooker. We were present when Iain, the senior manager of the group, kicked off a two-day meeting.

Iain arrived with a sheaf of dog-eared papers, apparently preparing to read his script aloud. The power of his communication that night, in our experience, has rarely been matched. Iain looked at his notes twice as he started speaking, and then, laying them aside, he continued passionately and earnestly for fifteen minutes, relating his deepest beliefs about leadership. He used imagery like Food TV's Emeril Lagasse uses spices. He declared that leaders were "not experts, but brokers" of skilled talent. He challenged his engineers with a Renaissance metaphor: "On a Michaelangelo scale of one to ten, we are somewhat further down the scale." He told his group that their creative genius needed to kick into gear or they would lose in the marketplace. To him, a best-in-class circuit design was a work of art. He expressed his belief in his group and their ability to win, finishing his speech to hearty applause.

Iain is a polished communicator and takes his communication abilities seriously, but it seemed to us at the time that his conviction and sincerity were what mattered most. He told us he believes the only way a manager should communicate with his team is to "tell it straight, simple, and with enthusiasm." A team member told us, "Iain doesn't need a circuit schematic to tell us what is important to him. He lives this leadership stuff every day. That's why we admire him. He feels so strongly about our work and us. Iain is, well, simply Iain."[1]

We trust, admire, and follow authentic and credible people, because we long to be authentic and credible ourselves. As role models, leaders are often symbols of our better selves—people we aspire to be like. We loathe phoniness and crave genuine leaders who truly stand for something, who believe in something.

There's a difference between a leader and a huckster. Hucksters tell great stories. Leaders tell their own story. The often-used phrase "find your voice" really means finding yourself—that is, the real you, the deeper you, the more meaningful you, or any other way you would like to express it. You have a voice—it may not have much power, because your self-knowledge may not be very strong. Psychologist Abraham Maslow observed that achieving authentic selfhood requires one "to know what one really wants or doesn't want, what one is fit for and what one is not fit for ... finding what your true self is and wants and in that process discovering your ability to lead."[2]

Finding your true self may not be all that easy, however. Some researchers and leadership theorists suggest it takes quite a few years of learning from good and bad experiences what your character is really like. As Abraham Zalesnik says, "Leaders grow through mastering painful conflict during their developmental years."[3] Some have likened the process of maturation to tempering steel—it requires tests of fire to become strong. Others have created a rich philosophical viewpoint that invites a leader to develop standards for the sake of personal excellence, to stand up to death and evil, and to work hard at identifying personal resistances to authenticity.[4]

For the past two decades leadership development has focused on competency and the metrically oriented feedback of 360-degree reports. These can be great aids in the process of becoming better acquainted with oneself. But as Manfred Kets de Vries observes, "Even aspects of our character—good as well as bad—can exist outside our awareness. Because we're equipped with a defensive structure that controls impulsive thoughts and ideas, we may not see our true character. We may not recognize the fact that something we routinely do rubs people the wrong way, for example—even if we leave burning heaps of irritation behind."[5]

That 360-degree feedback may expose some of these character blind spots, or they may be missed altogether. Some leaders may not care—all they want is for the work to get done. Those who are less willing to expand their own self-awareness, their own sense of self, can still get a great deal accomplished. But they remain stuck with a never-increasing capacity to use their voice—or worse, they increasingly lose their authentic voice and their ability to persuade. This may lead them to resort to power and other sources of mandate to get things done. This is the road to leadership disengagement.

Self-Mastery

Coming to grips with oneself is a lifelong effort. Knowing yourself, living with that knowledge, and disclosing it without defense, camouflage, or pretense is the essence of authenticity. Leading often promotes accelerated emotional maturation. It can also lead to self-destruction. The person who leads will hear power's seductive call and on a daily basis will confront the need to remain credible. Leadership invites us to confront our fears, our flaws, our beliefs about authority, and the quality of our relationships. Leaders are buffeted by undeserved criticism, lulled by unearned praise, and frustrated by the difficulty of getting things done through others' efforts.

A person can only rise above the trivial if they aspire to accomplish things that matter. Our aims must have some significance, or else we are doomed to continually ask, "Is this all there is?" Peter Koestenbaum argues that personal distinction is the direct result of a good leadership strategy colliding with authentic development. At the end of a daylong lecture, Boyd asked this business philosopher, "So, Peter, what is the meaning of life?"

Peter answered without hesitation, "It is to become mature."

"Exactly what do you mean, mature?"

Holding up a clenched fist, Peter said, "Mature people have a strong sense of self. They know who they are, what they believe in, confident in their opinions and judgment." He held up his other hand in an open, relaxed gesture. "They also have a humility that helps them continue to listen and learn; they care about other human beings and are willing to serve. When you are both of these at the same time, you are mature."[6] While not all authentic people are mature, all mature people are authentic. Have you ever worked for a jerk? Have you ever been a jerk? Jerks can be authentic, but never mature.

Fear of confrontation or self-revelation can diminish confidence, motivation, the ability to acquire and maintain relationships, and the ability to lead. There are many commonly shared and rather ordinary fears that shape our anxieties. These fears are pervasive across cultures and time, but are regularly mastered by those who are willing to confront them. We are afraid of looking bad, being judged, being found out, being rejected, and simply not being liked. Fear is the slave master of deception. Unhealthy needs are fear's partners in self-destruction. We need to be liked, gain control, have power, possess wealth, look perfect, become famous, or command admiration. These needs and fears create resistance to self-mastery or maturity. Some of these trace back to childhood trauma or other psychodynamic origins.

A simple method of evaluating your level of self-mastery is to imagine you are an airplane preparing to take off. Basic aerodynamics indicates there are four forces you must contend with to achieve and maintain flight. The two forces holding you back are weight and drag. The two forces that will overcome these are lift and thrust. This is a simple analogy for considering how to achieve a greater level of self-mastery—how to become a more aware, authentic, and mature leader. So ask yourself questions like:

- What is weighing me down?
- What unwanted weight do I carry that bogs me down as a leader?
- What holds me back from being the best version of myself?
- Do I know the answers to these tough questions?
- What do I really need to do to find out?

Alternatively, ask yourself what it is that gives lift to your leadership:

- What are my real aspirations?
- What are the things I want to accomplish as a leader that are beyond just personal and financial success?
- What legacy would I like to leave behind?
- And what assets do I have that give my leadership thrust, power, and more energy?
- What assets do I need to acquire that would provide more power?

A colleague, who for most of his life had had a strong need to be liked, told how he woke up one morning shortly after his fortieth birthday and realized he just didn't care very much about what other people thought of him. He described a profoundly liberating feeling of being free to be himself. For years he had tried to be what everyone else wanted him to be rather than being himself. He felt he had had to camouflage his real self and worked hard at being liked rather than authentically himself. It turned out his real self was more genuinely appreciated and pretty terrific. People respected him and followed him despite occasional irritations caused by those little parts of his character he used to subdue. His need to be liked had been causing more weight and drag than he realized.

As we relinquish the quest for who we think we should be and discover who we actually are, genuineness and vulnerability emerge as new and comfortable friends. The key to transforming our organizations—and ourselves—is to stop pretending. Embrace the uncomfortable truth and change the things that drag you down or hold you back.

The Ability to Be Believed

Credibility is the condition of being believable. It is linked with reputation, status, and legitimacy. The word itself comes from two words: *credo,* meaning, "I believe," and ability. The word *credo* is the root word for "credentials," "creed," and "credit." When it comes to leadership communication, a common expression heard around the world is "walking your talk." Those who are most trusted and most heard are those whose walk and talk are not just devoid of deception but also stand for something important. Our ability to walk our talk demands an integration of voice and behavior. When we choose to lead, our voice and actions speak our intentions.

Three important aspects that constituents evaluate when judging a person's leadership credibility are morality/ethics, intentions, and competence. In most of the relationships in our lives, morality/ethics and intentions are the prime indicators. In business, competence assumes equal status and is often the leading indicator. Competence is expressed both in our technical ability and in our interpersonal ability. The impact of your voice rises and falls dramatically based on the ability to communicate, because it is linked directly to constituents' willingness to trust—to find you credible. The message is never evaluated outside the messenger. Your voice and credibility are inseparably linked.

When you hide behind a facade, stay safe, or keep your emotional distance, others, not knowing who you really are, filter what you say. They may do this to protect themselves, or to discount your leadership, or both. The reverberating cry for more communication often expresses the need of constituents to connect with those leaders who remain distant. In some cases, more communication actually makes things worse. When leaders communicate more but are not trusted, it simply provides the organization with more things not to believe. The cry for more communication is often the symptom of the undiagnosed disease—mistrust. The disease is cured with **authentic** communication, not more communication.

Psychologists know that most people enter into trust with relative ease and that some find trust difficult. Most groups are made up of both types of people. Psychologists refer to those who are willing and able to trust easily as "high-trusters" and those more wary or less able to trust as "low-trusters." When leaders communicate messages that spur internal competitiveness, the "high-trusters" tend to be okay, but the trust level for the wary or "low-trusters" decreases. Internal competition and competitive messages (messages aimed at getting internal groups to compete against each other) cause the disengaged and wary to trust less. Messages of cooperation increase trust among the "high-trusters." Cooperation messages may not increase trust with "low-trusters," but it doesn't cause their low levels of trust to sink any lower. And for these people, this may be as good as it gets.

The greatest threat to inspiring trust is sending inconsistent messages. Inconsistency causes trust to plummet for both the "high-trusters" and "low-trusters." Cooperative and consistent messages secure the greatest level of trust.[7]

Acceptable Flaws

In the heat of crisis or with the sustained pressure of time, hidden flaws will be revealed and the leader can lose trust, along with goodwill and loyalty. But when a leader is authentic, constituents are willing to look past his or her acceptable flaws. Flaws make us human, more accessible, even more endearing, and within reasonable boundaries we readily forgive and even embrace some flaws. We are talking about the kind of flaws that add to our character, not character flaws. No one expects you to be the perfect role model, but they do expect to see a close connection between who you profess to be and who you really are.

We have often encountered authentic and credible leaders who have gained loyalty even when they possess lesser amounts of other important leadership traits. We came across such a situation while working in upstate New York several years ago. We were attending a leadership conference with a client at a historic location on a forested hilltop along the Hudson River. We were meeting with a group of executives from a multi-billion dollar leading-edge company. During an afternoon break, we were on the lawn with one of the participants, deep in conversation about his frustrations with his boss.

"What is your opinion of him?" we asked.

"In confidence?" he asked while looking over the top of his glasses.

"Of course," we replied.

"Okay," he said, "I'll tell you. I think the guy is obsessed with status, loves to micro-manage, and doesn't give two cents about how I feel about the situation."

"Sounds tough," we said, "so why do you work so hard for him?"

"Well, this may sound funny, but even though he is a son-of-a-bitch, he's brilliant. He's nearly always right, he's on top of things, and I'm learning a great deal from him. We don't like each other, really, but I always know where I stand with the guy. Sometimes he's a jerk, and often he doesn't seem to care, but he lets you know that up front. I guess I admire his genuineness. He is who he is, no hidden agenda or pretense. And if my performance matches expectations, I get the credit and the rewards. He's a tough but fair boss. It's funny—I don't like him, but I respect him."

This leader has maturity's closed fist but not its open hand, and still must learn to respect and serve others. Yet even though his maturity is stunted, followers responded to his authenticity. Authentic jerks are preferable to phony glad-handers.

Stories like this tend to add up over the years and form an observable pattern. In fact, we have been asking middle and frontline leaders about their former role models and those role models' communication abilities for years. The following quotes capture the spirit of what they have said:

"The guy simply told us like it was, in plain English."

"I knew what she was saying was true, because I'd watched her live her words."

"She wasn't afraid to let you know where she stood, show her true self."

"Even when the company was lying, we trusted him to tell the truth."

These people are describing leaders who do not cover the truth. It is far more often the cover-up, not the foul-up, that crashes careers. Many well-intentioned business leaders, in an attempt to hold things together and keep things moving, make a dreadful leadership mistake. Whether out of an unconscious fear or deliberate malice, they dance around the truth and ask others to join them on the dance floor.

This dancing collusion causes leaders and followers to publicly pretend to believe one thing while each privately believes something different. Sometimes the dance is a quick Texas two-step; sometimes it's a long, passionate tango. We dance to avoid conflict. We dance because we need to be liked. We dance because we want to manipulate others. We dance because we are in some way afraid of the truth and the emotions the truth may stimulate in others. It happens when leaders and followers trade difficult truths for comfortable falsehoods, dangerous issues for safer ones, or a messy reality for a tidy make-believe.

These dangerous dances create lasting problems. As Chris Argyris points out, even if the deception has momentary positive consequences, darker forces are at work. "In the name of maintaining a good working relationship, all parties bypassed [the truth] and then covered up their bypass. The inevitable result: inner contradictions remain and frustration grows. Thus, gaps and inconsistencies are not just problems of logic or argument. They are a recipe, a tested recipe, for bickering, dysfunctional behavior, and lackluster performance."[8]

Every time your team avoids the critical "real issue," you lose. Every time the discussion outside the meeting room, physical or virtual, is dramatically different from the discussion inside the room, you lose. Many leaders are unable to believe in others simply because they do not believe in themselves. Deceiving ourselves and deluding others damages trust and condemns business leaders to losing their voice.

Authenticity Is Your Megaphone

Authenticity—credibility combined with passion—is a leader's megaphone. It amplifies the message above the clamor of downsizing or acquisitions, the whining of Wall Street, and the screams of competitors. Without authenticity, the facts, emotions, and symbols a leader communicates are dialed down.

The journey to greater authenticity begins when you identify the difference between what you believe and the truths you have inherited from others. Authentic leaders are more focused, centered, integrated, self-directing, and purposeful. Their need for approval, acceptance, status, deference, and even money diminishes as authenticity increases. Authentic leaders are dedicated to work that matters.

Authenticity liberates and relaxes. It requires much less energy to maintain balance. A leader's vulnerability stimulates courage in others and grants constituents permission to be themselves and speak the truth. Barriers dissolve and communication flows. Acts of authenticity are ultimately acts of faith in your constituency. If you do not believe in yourself, it becomes difficult to believe in others. Doubting ourselves and deceiving others undermines all leadership ability and abolishes voice. "Everything you do in relation to other people causes them to make judgments about what you stand for and what your message is. '**You are the message**' comes down to the fact that unless you identify yourself as a walking, talking message, you miss that critical point."[9]

Vision: Lifting the Fog

Have you ever driven suddenly into a fog bank? You immediately slow down, gripping the steering wheel more tightly as you become more alert to dangers. If others are traveling with you, you shush their conversation. You instinctively try your bright lights, even though doing so didn't work the last ten times. You turn the radio down so you can see better. You crane your neck over the steering wheel in an attempt to see a few centimeters farther into the fog. You scan for the stripes or roadside reflectors that provide guidance. You frantically check the rearview mirror, worried your own taillights will not be seen. The longer you drive in the fog, the more fatigued you become. Your perception of time alters. At some point your mind can only focus on wanting to get out of the fog.

This is a one-to-one matching metaphor for the research on the lack of vision in organizations. When people are in the fog, they report more personal job stress. Productivity dips (they slow down). People reduce their interactions with others (outside gossiping and complaining about the fog). Workers become far more sensitive to dangers that might hurt them, such as redundancy, unexpected performance indicators, or unnecessary or misunderstood reorganization. Constituents, straining to see the stripes on the road, cry out for more communication, more clarity.

As we have already described in chapter 2, humans view the future along with the past and present to create a coherent story. Present and future uncertainties produce fog. Without this future story, the organization defaults to the tedium of checklists, tense workers keeping their eyes fixed on blurry road stripes. Everyone is relieved when the fog lifts.

"He who predicts the future lies even if he tells the truth" is an Arab proverb worth repeating.[10] **Predicting** the future is a hazardous avocation, but inspiring the hearts and minds of constituents to pursue a worthy goal is an inescapable leadership task. Constituents expect leaders to both describe and inspire the desire to reach a commendable destination, and to foster confidence that the strategic route in hand is the best path to this destination. The leader's job is to build a shared image of the future, foster commitment, and orchestrate alignment.

This past, present, and future story combines two common leadership ideas. The story must describe the vision of the future, which is the search for meaning. But future meaning is always evaluated against values of the past and present. Why are we going to this destination? What is meaningful, admirable, or enviable about traveling to this destination rather than a different one? The story must also describe the strategy, which is the search for advantage. What is the best way to get there? If obstacles occur, do we have alternate routes we can take?

Understand the Past

"Without understanding who we have been and what it has meant, it is difficult to reconceive where we are going or ought to go."[11] Leaders link the symbolic past to the uncertain future. Begin by answering the question "What is our claim to greatness?" Understanding our historical greatness gives us confidence. Timelines, lists, storyboards, and other historical representations capture corporate events, stories, and people. Purpose, inspiration, and meaning are communicated through these records. Strategies, achievements, and the ability to cope with change are also conveyed. Consider the symbolic past with an eye toward the story it tells.

Analyze the Present

Examining trends, assessing competitive and technological threats, benchmarking best practices, evaluating a balanced scorecard, and taking the pulse of the organization's vital signs are techniques for analyzing the present. While analyzing the present, leaders are enticed to consider that all other parts of the coherent story are intact, so concentrating their message on immediate and urgent details is their most important communication activity. This is a deception. Repetition of the coherent story at a much higher frequency than seems necessary is often required for the present urgencies to make sense against the coherent story.

Inspire Others about the Future

Most vision and mission statements are a bland statement of general, multiple intentions such as "leading the industry," "being employer of choice," or "we are cooler than they are." Superior vision statements tend to connect with enduring stories like LensCrafters' "Gift of Sight," or TNT's "We Know Drama."

However, vision statements are not the vision, just like maps are not the territory. The goal is not to laminate the vision, but to provide direction, unite, and inspire others to believe in the coherent story. Vision is the future-perfect part of this story. It describes why the ordeals and successes of the past and present will be worth the continued effort.

Connect Strategy and Vision

Once strategies are selected, they must be communicated as part of the whole story, not as a separate story. Deciding upon strategic direction is so critical, and requires such a great deal of time and effort, that as leaders define an organization's direction, they often rush toward implementation communication—that is, orders. This gives rise to the four fatal assumptions of communication that we discussed earlier. Traveling a route only makes sense if the route is going somewhere. If leaders only communicate about the stripes on the road, and ask people to measure their progress by counting stripes, over time constituents will begin to ask, "Where are we going?" If the only answer is couched in more stripe counting, the coherent story disassembles and fog appears.

Unite the Organization

Uniting a group to see and believe in a central movie is the task of aligning hearts and minds to the coherent story. This is the responsibility of leaders, aided by, but not replaced by, the marketing or communication department. Using techniques borrowed from processes such as brand management, storyboarding, metaphor development, and screen writing, a leader must consider the factual, emotional, and symbolic components of the story.

It is like making a movie of the company's history and destiny that helps constituents see themselves as the action stars. By creating a rich plot, leaders can include customers, employees, shareholders, and partners in the same movie. Hollywood director Sidney Lumet has always maintained that the best movies are made when everyone—screenwriters, electricians, directors, actors, lighting specialists, key grips, best boys, and cutting room technicians—work to make the **same movie.** He recounts a memorable moment from his experience of shooting *The Seagull* in Sweden. The crew was deep in the woods, lighting a night scene.

> An hour after nightfall, I drove out to the set. The road led over a hill. As the car came over the crest, I saw below me a small, concentrated, white-hot diamond. Everything around it was black except for this beautiful burst of light, where the set was being lit. It's a sight I'll always remember: people working so hard, all making the same movie, creating, literally, a picture in the middle of a forest in the middle of the night.[12]

Many leaders we have worked with have had moments such as these in their careers. It is a deeply satisfying and often profitable experience to see all constituents engaged in doing the best work of their lives. Vision is a love affair with an idea. And, like love, it needs to be communicated in both small and big ways. Vision messages in a distributed network require simplicity and frequency to pierce an organization's natural static. The message must be simple to flow easily through the network. Repetition fosters remembrance, so leaders should speak often.

Maintaining Connection

Humans congregate. We create tribes, teams, communities, and nations. We stay connected via face-to-face encounters and through a myriad of low-tech and high-tech virtual communication techniques and systems. The rise of social networks via Internet and cell phone use is a modern expression of the human need to get and stay connected.

Staying connected with people is one of the fundamentals of leadership. Leadership involves relationships. The rise of social intelligence and emotional intelligence as key aspects of connecting and maintaining connections with others is not surprising. In the mid-1980s Howard Gardner hypothesized that leadership was a subset of interpersonal intelligence. In the late 1990s researchers reported the effects of maintaining connection in a virtual world. "Fundamentally, emotional connection is important because it leads to goodwill. In turn, employees give leaders the benefit of the doubt on difficult matters, put forth their best efforts, and make sacrifices. In global organizations with webs of interrelated units that must cooperate and coordinate to meet customer needs, goodwill—rather than clear lines of command and control—is what leaders need to achieve global initiatives."[13]

Today there is a bounty of books and research about this subject of connection, whether it goes by the classification of "emotional intelligence," "interpersonal skills," "social intelligence," or any one of several proposed labels. The evidence basically supports two facts. The first of these is that the vitality of an organization is commensurate with connection. "The ability of organizations to reach their next level of greatness is determined by the atmosphere. The atmosphere is determined by the quality of the relationships. The quality of the relationships is determined by the quality of the conversations and behaviors."[14]

The second fact is that the task of creating, maintaining, and leading connection is exhausting and confounding. In our race to use resources around the globe, we have come to realize that what a person can do is more important than where they work. Add to this virtual work style a reduction of hierarchical status and better power distribution throughout organizations, and you get virtual, networked companies. Most of us feel the empowerment of these new structures while we also feel the tugs of disconnection they perpetrate. Richard Boyatzis and Annie McKee, coauthors with Daniel Goleman on work concerning social intelligence, have written about the difficulty of maintaining connection in their own book. They use the term "resonance" to express the idea that leaders create these powerful, vibrant, and positive atmospheres of organizational connection. "Even the best leaders—those who **can** create resonance—must give of themselves constantly. For many people, especially the busy executives we work with, little value is placed on **renewal**, or developing practices—habits of mind, body, and behavior—that enable us to create and sustain resonance in the face of unending challenges, year in and year out. In fact it is often just the opposite. Many organizations overvalue certain kinds of destructive behavior and tolerate discord and mediocre leadership for a very long time."[15]

Connection and Self-Renewal

The need for creating and maintaining connection is thwarted by our own predilection to get the job done on an efficient cost basis. From a communications point of view, this far too often means sitting in an office, in an airplane seat, or in a hotel room somewhere in the world banging out emails by the score. The emotional channel is strangled by the lack of visual or auditory cues that face-to-face conversation provides (whether done in person or via videoconference). Although managing without email today is literally inconceivable, it's an unfortunate fact that many managers haven't developed, or choose not to develop, more relationship-oriented sensibilities like knowing when picking up the phone is far superior to several days of frustrating email exchanges.

These two ideas—learning to connect and learning to renew—are core to maintaining voice. While emotional or social disconnection does not cause as immediate or perhaps as damaging a loss of voice as does a loss of credibility or vision, the effects can nevertheless range from bad to disastrous. Helping leaders learn how to better connect is the job of leadership development.

Fortunately, the rise of leadership development as a necessary competence for organizational survival is encouraging, but it is not universal. And even though billions of dollars are spent each year on leadership development, most of those dollars are directed at managers who are preparing for larger leadership positions, not at those who are already in middle or senior leadership positions. Some people believe social intelligence can be taught. Others do not. Still others take the middle ground. If you believe interpersonal or social intelligence skills cannot be learned or improved over time, then your task as a leader is to continuously search for the gifted minority who naturally possess these abilities. If you feel that emotional and social intelligence **can** be improved over time, **then** your task is different—invest in methods that will increase the quotient of these abilities in your organization. Your current and future success depends upon doing so. And communication as a corporate problem will decrease by association.

In terms of renewal, several authorities weigh in on this subject. Former CEO, educator, and psychologist Richard Farson suggests the following:

> We all tend to like people we do things for more than people we do things to, or people who only do things for us. And we like people more when we do not feel victimized by them. That's

why better managers can do both: be generous with their time and energy, and yet be quick to confront an employee whose behavior is victimizing. They realize that the problem is not in raising the morale of the work force; if anything, it is in raising their own morale as managers. If their morale is high, eventually they are more likely to develop a more creative and enthusiastic work force.[16]

Boyd Clarke and John W. Gardner used words and ideas that still affect me. Boyd used to always tell me that leadership work was hard, thankless, and a joy on any given day. He and I used to joke, complain, and revel about our own struggles as leaders as we helped so many others develop communication skills. On several occasions I asked him what kept him going, and he nearly always answered by saying, "I love this work and can think of no better contribution to the future of this planet than increasing the supply of leaders in the world." He dedicated his work life to understanding how to do this and devoted his craft as an educator, counselor, and coach to helping leaders renew their leadership vows. Boyd's thoughts are amplified by Gardner's views. In his book Self-Renewal, Gardner stated, "First and last, humans live by ideas that validate their striving, ideas that say it's worth living and trying. What makes a collection of people a society is the cohesiveness that stems out of shared values, purposes and beliefs."[17]

Your job as a leader is to use your love of your own work to light the fire of passion in others who share this love. Connect your voice to this well of passion, and you will never be at a loss for words that will incite action.

NOTES

Introduction

1 Claudio Fernández-Aráoz, "Getting the Right People at the Top," Sloan *Management Review* 46, no. 4 (summer 2005).

2 George Bernard Shaw, "Trivia," TV.com, http://www.tv.com/george-bernard-shaw/person/173281/trivia.html.

3 George Bernard Shaw, "Maxims for Revolutionists," in the play Man and Superman (1903).

Chapter 1: The Case for Communication

1 Chip Heath and Dan Heath, *Made to Stick: Why Some Ideas Survive and Others Die* (New York: Random House, 2007), 34.

2 Learning International, "Strategic Vision: A New Role for Corporate Leaders" (Stamford, CT: Learning International, Inc., 1986), 40.

3 "Executive Vision Communication," author's research, 1989.

4 Marcus Buckingham and Curt Coffman, *First Break All The Rules: What the World's Greatest Managers Do Differently* (New York: Simon & Schuster, 1999), 33.

5 "Employees Cite Poor Managers as Primary Reason for Quitting," PR Newswire, eCruiting, Inc., January 28, 2002, http://www.ecruitinginc.com/news/news.asp?ID=360, accessed November 6, 2007.

6 Author's research, online poll, November 2002.

7 Jim Shaffer, *The Leadership Solution* (New York: McGraw Hill, 2000), 4.

8 "New Research Shows Executives Lack the 'Gift of Gab,'" Online Recruitment, October 12, 2003, http://www.onrec.com/content2/news.asp?ID=3316, accessed November 6, 2007.

9 "Only One-Third of Companies Say Their Employees Understand and Live Business Strategy in Daily Jobs," International Association of Business Communicators, September 13, 2005, http://news.iabc.com/index.php?s=press_releases&item=19, accessed November 6, 2007.

10 "Seven Common Leadership Complaints from CEOs," *Chief Learning Officer,* October 2007, http://www.clomedia.com/in-the-news/2007/October/1971/index.php, accessed November 9, 2007.

11 Shaffer, *Leadership Solution*, 4.

12 *Ibid.*

13 Donald N. Sull and Charles Spinosa, "Promise-Based Management: The Essence of Execution," *Harvard Business Review* 85, no. 4 (April 2007): 81.

14 *Ibid.*

15 Ibid., 86.

16 Georgianne Smith, "Emotional, Symbolic, and Factual Dimensions of Leadership Communication," unpublished dissertation, Pepperdine University, August 1977, 89.

17 Ping Ping Fu, et al., "The Impact of Societal Cultural Values and Individual Social Beliefs on the Perceived Effectiveness of Managerial Influence Strategies," *Journal of International Business Studies* 35, no. 4 (July 2004): 289.

18 *Ibid.*, 300.

19 James A. Winchester, "The Effect of Symbolic and Factual Content on Leader Communications," unpublished dissertation, Pepperdine University, August 1997, 72.

20 Howard Gardner, *Leading Minds: An Anatomy of Leadership* (New York: Basic Books, 1995), 34.

Chapter 2: Your Brain on Communication

1 Antonio Damasio, *Descartes' Error: Emotion, Reason, and the Human Brain* (New York: Grosset/Putnam, 1994), 31.

2 *Ibid.*, 33<N>51.

3 Oliver Sacks, The Man Who Mistook His Wife for a Hat: and Other Clinical Tales (New York: HarperPerennial, 1970), 177<N>86.

4 *Ibid.*, 183<N>84; italics in original.

5 *Ibid.*, 184.

6 John H. Ratey, *A User's Guide to the Brain: Perception, Attention, and the Four Theaters of the Brain* (New York: Vintage, 2002), 5.

7 Joseph LeDoux, *The Emotional Brain: The Mysterious Underpinnings of Emotional Life* (New York: Touchstone, 1996), 33.

8 V. S. Ramachandran, *A Brief Tour of Human Consciousness: From Imposter Poodles to Purple Numbers* (New York: Pi Press, 2004), 96.

9 Antonio Damasio, *Looking for Spinoza: Joy, Sorrow, and the Feeling Brain* (Orlando, FL: Harcourt, 2003), 198.

10 Ratey, *User's Guide*, 5.

11   Damasio, *Looking for Spinoza,* 194.

12   Richard S. Lazarus and Bernice N. Lazarus, *Passion and Reason: Making Sense of Our Emotions* (New York: Oxford University Press, 1996), 199.

13   LeDoux, *Emotional Brain,* 19.

14   Ratey, *User's Guide,* 186.

15   Damasio, *Looking for Spinoza,* 195.

16   LeDoux, *Emotional Brain,* 106.

17   Ian Tattersall, "Drenched in Symbolism," *Scientific American* 281, no. 1 (July 2003): 55.

18   George Lakoff and Mark Johnson, *Metaphors We Live By* (Chicago: University of Chicago Press, 1980), 257.

19   Gardner, *Leading Minds,* 65.

20   Steven Pinker, *How the Mind Works* (New York: W. W. Norton, 1996), 359.

21   Antonio Damasio, *The Feeling of What Happens: Body and Emotion in the Making of Consciousness* (New York: Harcourt Brace, 1999), 189.

22   Matt Ridley, *Nature Via Nurture: Genes, Experience, and What Makes Us Human* (New York: HarperCollins, 2003), 220.

23   Pinker, *How the Mind Works,* 552.

24   Quoted in Jessica Snyder Sachs, "A Spielberg in Your Own Mind," *Popular Science,* July 2003, 52.

25   Ratey, *User's Guide,* 186.

26   *Ibid.*

27   Robert McKee, "Storytelling That Moves People," *Harvard Business Review* 81, no. 6 (June 2003): 52.

28   William Shakespeare, *MacBeth* 5.5.19<N>28 (London: Wordsworth Editions, 2005), 97<N>98.

Chapter 3: The Central Movie

1   Quotes from the matching quiz come from a variety of online sources: Ho Chi Mihn, Mahatma Gandhi, Tony Blair, Mao Zedong, Bill Clinton, and Ernesto "Che" Guevara, http://thinkexist.com/quotes; Mother Teresa, Ronald Reagan, Margaret Thatcher, Martin Luther King Jr., Boris Yeltsin, and Nelson Mandela, http://www.brainyquote.com; John F. Kennedy and Winston Churchill, http://www. quotationspage.com/quotes; and Aung San Suu Kyi, http://www.inform.com/Aung+San_Suu_Kyi,Canada. All sources were accessed October 27, 2007.

2   "Bye-bye Boris," *Economist,* April 23, 2007, 93.

3   Sidney Lumet, *Making Movies* (New York: Vintage Books, 1996), 218.

4   Howard Gardner, *Changing Minds: The Art and Science of Changing Our Own and Other People's Minds* (Boston: Harvard Business School Press, 2004), 15<N>18.

5   "A History of the Olympics," About.com, http://history1900s.about. com/library/weekly/aa081000a.htm; and "Pierre de Coubertin," International Olympic Committee, http://www.olympic.org/uk/ passion/museum/permanent/coubertin/index_uk.asp, accessed November 28, 2007.

6   "Organisation," International Olympic Committee, http://www.olympic.org/uk/organisation/index_uk.asp, accessed November 28, 2007.

7   Bob Chambers, personal interview, May 7, 2002.

8   Scott Givens, personal interviews, March 12 and 27, 2002.

9   Haven Riviere, personal interview, April 8, 2002.

10   "Legacies of North American Games—Salt Lake," Vancouver Organizing Committee for the 2010 Olympic and Paralympic Winter Games, http://www.vancouver2010.com/en/ OrganizingCommittee/PublicCommunications/Reports/ LastingLegaciesSaltLake, accessed November 28, 2007.

11   *Ibid.*

12   "Games-Related Economic Development Numbers," *Deseret News,* March 2, 2002.

13   Lisa Riley Roche, "Games Surplus No $80 Million," *Deseret News,* April 22, 2002.

14   "Games-Related Economic Development."

15   Bill Pennington, "2002 Games: Riveting Sport and Angry Backlash," *New York Times,* February 24, 2002. Available at http://query.nytimes. com/gst/fullpage.html?res=9E05E4D81E3EF937A15751C0A9649C8B6, accessed November 28, 2007.

Chapter 4: TNT and Lenscrafters

1   TNT: personal interviews with Steve Koonin, Scot Safon, and Jennifer Dorian, February and April 2002. Subsequent quotes from the 2004 Tom Peters Company video case study.

2   LensCrafters: personal interview with Dave Browne, April 8 and 9, 2002. Information on current Luxottica retail stores and mission statement from its Web site.

Chapter 5: Symbols and Stories

1. Judy S. DeLoache, "Mindful of Symbols," *Scientific American,* July 2005, 51.

2   "Judy S. DeLoache," University of Virginia faculty page, http://www.faculty.virginia.edu/deloache, accessed November 21, 2007.

3   "Origins of Sayings: When in Rome, Do as the Romans Do," Trivia-Library.com, http://www.trivia-library.com/b/ origins-of-sayings-when-in-rome-do-as-the-romans-do.htm, and "Cliches and Expressions Origins," www.businessballs.com, both accessed November 26, 2007.

4   Tattersall, "Drenched in Symbolism," 62.

5   Steven J. Mithen, *The Prehistory of the Mind: The Cognitive Origins of Art, Religion, and Science* (London: Thames and Hudson, 1996), 26.

6   Lakoff and Johnson, *Metaphors We Live By,* 55; italics in original.

7   Pinker, How the Mind Works, 359.

8   Susan Oyama, *Evolution's Eye: A Systems View of the Biology-Culture Divide* (Durham, NC: Duke University Press, 2000), 10.

9   Cristina B. Gibson and Mary E. Zellmer-Bruhn, "Metaphors and Meaning: An Intercultural Analysis of the Concept of Teamwork," *Administrative Science Quarterly,* July 2001, http://findarticles.com/p/articles/mi_m4035/is_2_46/ai_79829823, accessed November 21, 2007.

10   Quoted in David Emery, "JFK: 'I Am a Jelly Doughnut,'" About.com: Urban Legends, http://urbanlegends.about.com/cs/ historical/a/jfk_berliner.htm, accessed November 26, 2007.

11   Terry Maxon, "The Chairman, Dr. McDreamy, Meets CEO Edna Turnblad," Airline Biz: Frivolity Archives, November 1, 2007, http://aviation.beloblog.com/archives/frivolity, accessed November 26, 2007.

12   "Charles Kettering Quotes," BrainyQuote, http://www.brainyquote.com/quotes/authors/c/charles_kettering.html, accessed November 26, 2007.

13   Mark Bernstein, *Grand Eccentrics: Turning the Century: Dayton and the Inventing of America* (Wilmington, OH: Orange Frazer Press, 1996), 75.

14   Lakoff and Johnson, Metaphors We Live By, 244.

15   Ted Kooser, *The Poetry Home Repair Manual: Practical Advice for Beginning Poets* (Lincoln: University of Nebraska Press, 2005), 126.

16   Damasio, *Feeling of What Happens,* 189.

17   Daniel J. Siegel, *The Developing Mind: How Relationships and the Brain Interact to Shape Who We Are* (New York: Guilford Press, 1999), 331.

18   Pascal Boyer, *Religion Explained: The Evolutionary Origins of Religious Thought* (New York: Basic Books, 2001), 83.

19   Robin Hogarth, *Educating Intuition* (Chicago: University of Chicago Press, 2001), 94<N>95.

20   Barry Lopez, *Crossing Open Ground* (1978; New York: Vintage Books, 1989), 70.

21   Douglas A. Ready, "How Storytelling Builds Next-Generation Leaders," *Sloan Management Review* 43, no. 4 (Summer 2002): 66.

22   Marilyn Carlson story originally from http://www.diversityjournal.com/ceospeeches/speech014.htm, accessed March 2002, and "Marilyn Carlson Nelson: Believe in the Power of One," online video, *Times* Online (UK), September 5, 2007, http://www.timesonline.co.uk/tol/life_and_style/career_and_jobs/article2392812.ece, accessed November 26, 2007.

23   Mark D. Carlson story, used with permission.

Chapter 6: Tune In to Emotions

1   "WLW," http://www.ominous-valve.com/wlw.html, accessed November 28, 2007.

2   Kathleen Hall-Jamieson, *Eloquence in an Electronic Age: The Transformation of Political Speechmaking* (1988; New York: Oxford University Press, 1990), 182.

3   Damasio, *Looking for Spinoza,* 48

4   Quoted in J. D. Mayer, D. Goleman, D. Barrett, et al., "Leading by Feel," *Harvard Business Review* 82, no. 1 (January 2004): 28.

5   Lazarus and Lazarus, *Passion and Reason,* 203.

6   LeDoux, *Emotional Brain,* 18.

7   Steven Johnson, *Mind Wide Open: Your Brain and the Neuroscience of Everyday Life* (New York: Scribner, 2004), 41.

8   Ron Crossland and Gregg Thompson, *The Leadership Experience: From Individual Success to Organizational Significance* (New York: Select Books, 2007), 53<N>56.

9   Dave Browne interview.

10   Daniel Goleman, Richard Boyatzis, and Annie McKee, "Primal Leadership: The Hidden Driver of Great Performance," *Harvard*

Business Review 79, no. 11 (December 2001): 51.

11 John Seely Brown and Paul Duguid, *The Social Life of Information* (Boston: Harvard Business School Press, 2000), 102.

12 Valerie Manusov and Miles L. Patterson, *The Sage Handbook of Nonverbal Communication* (Thousand Oaks, CA: Sage Publications, 2006), 86.

Chapter 7: The Altar of Data

1   "Ivan Pavlov Quotes," BrainyQuotes, http://www.brainyquote.com/quotes/authors/i/ivan_pavlov.html, accessed December 3, 2007.

2   Joel Best, *Damned Lies and Statistics: Untangling Numbers from the Media, Politicians, and Activists* (Berkeley: University of California Press, 2001).

3   "John Allen Paulos and the Sporadic Exponent," John Allen Paulos home page, http://www.math.temple.edu/~paulos, accessed December 3, 2007.

4   John Allen Paulos, *A Mathematician Reads the Newspaper* (New York: Basic Books, 1995), 81.

5   Chip Heath and Dan Heath, *Made to Stick: Why Some Ideas Survive and Others Die* (New York: Random House, 2007).

6   Brooks Jackson and Kathleen Hall-Jamieson, *UnSpun: Finding Facts in a World of Disinformation* (New York: Random House, 2007), x, xi.

7   Harrison "Buzz" Price, *Walt's Revolution! By the Numbers* (Orlando, FL: Ripley Entertainment, 2004).

8   Harrison "Buzz" Price interview by Geoff Thatcher.

9   Kathleen O'Toole, "What Makes Some Ideas Hang Around," *Stanford Business* 70, no. 2 (February 2002): 35.

10 Thomas Peluso, personal interview, 1996.

11 "The History of a Picture's Worth," http://www2.cs.uregina.ca/~hepting/research/web/words/history.html, accessed December 3, 2007.

12 Lou Gilligan, personal interview, June 1992.

13 Scott Rosenberg, "The Data Artist," Salon.com, March 10, 1997, 2, http://www.salon.com/march97/tufte2970310.html, accessed December 3, 2007.

14 Don Pierce, personal interviews, June 1996 and March 10, 2002.

15 "List of Rivers by Length," Wikipedia.com, http://en.wikipedia.org/wiki/List_of_rivers_by_length, accessed December 3, 2007.

16 "List of Tallest Buildings and Structures in the World," Wikipedia.com,

http://en.wikipedia.org/wiki/Tallest_building, accessed December 3, 2007.

17   "The Cure for Insomnia," Wikipedia.com, http://en.wikipedia.org/wiki/The_Cure_for_Insomnia, accessed December 3, 2007.

18   Eric H. Chudler, "Amazing Animal Senses," Neuroscience for Kids, December 5, 2007, http://faculty.washington.edu/chudler/amaze.html, accessed December 5, 2007.

19   Paulos, *Mathematician Reads the Newspaper*, 81.

20   Best, *Damned Lies and Statistics*, 4.

21   ProCon.org, http://www.procon.org/franklinletter.htm, accessed December 5, 2007. Original source: Whitfield J. Bell and Leonard W. Labaree, ed., *Mr. Franklin: A Selection from His Personal Letters* (New Haven, CT: Yale University Press, 1956).

22   "When to Take My Name Off the Door," Leo Burnett, World of Biography, http://www.worldofbiography.com/9129-Leo%20Burnett/valedictionaddress.htm, accessed December 5, 2007.

Chapter 8: Losing Your Voice

1   Iain Morris, personal interview, May 1994.

2   Quoted in Jay Alden Conger, *Learning to Lead: The Art of Transforming Managers into Leaders* (San Francisco: Jossey-Bass, 1992), 57.

3   Quoted in *ibid.*, 25.

4   Peter Koestenbaum, *Leadership: The Innerside of Greatness; A Philosophy for Leaders* (San Francisco: Jossey-Bass, 2002), 20.

5   Manfred Kets de Vries, *The Leadership Mystique: A User's Manual for the Human Enterprise* (London: Financial Times/Prentice Hall, 2001), 14.

6   Peter Koestenbaum, personal interview, May 16, 1992.

7   Roderick M. Kramer, "Trust and Distrust in Organizations: Emerging Perspective, Enduring Questions," *Annual Review of Psychology* 50 (1999): 569<N>98.

8   Chris Argyris, *Flawed Advice and the Management Trap: How Managers Can Know When They're Getting Good Advice and When They're Not* (New York: Oxford University Press, 2000), 51.

9   Roger Ailes, with Jon Kraushar, *You Are The Message: Getting What You Want by Being Who You Are* (New York: Doubleday, 1988), 25.

10   Peter Schwartz, *The Art of the Long View: Planning for the Future in an Uncertain World* (New York: Doubleday, 1996), 6.

11   Hall-Jamieson, *Eloquence in an Electronic Age*, 239.

12   Lumet, *Making Movies*, 36.

13 Hal B. Gregersen, Allen J. Morrison, and J. Stewart Black, "Developing Leaders for the Global Frontier," *Sloan Management Review* 40, no. 1 (Fall 1998): 24.

14 Judith E. Glaser, *The DNA of Leadership: Leverage Your Instincts to Communicate-Differentiate-Innovate* (Avon, MA: Platinum Press, 2006), 17.

15 Richard Boyatzis and Annie McKee, *Resonant Leadership: Renewing Yourself and Connecting with Others Through Mindfulness, Hope, and Compassion* (Boston: Harvard Business School Press, 2005), 5.

16 Richard Farson, *Management of the Absurd: Paradoxes in Leadership* (New York: Touchstone, 1997), 143.

17 John W. Gardner, *Self-Renewal: The Individual and the Innovative Society* (New York: W. W. Norton, 1981), xiii-xiv.

SELECT BIBLIOGRAPHY

Ailes, Roger, with Jon Kraushar. *You Are The Message: Getting What You Want by Being Who You Are.* New York: Doubleday, 1988.

Argyris, Chris. *Flawed Advice and the Management Trap: How Managers Can Know When They're Getting Good Advice and When They're Not.* New York: Oxford University Press, 2000.

Best, Joel. *Damned Lies and Statistics: Untangling Numbers from the Media, Politicians, and Activists.* Berkeley: University of California Press, 2001.

Boyatzis, Richard, and Annie McKee. *Resonant Leadership: Renewing Yourself and Connecting with Others Through Mindfulness, Hope, and Compassion.* Boston: Harvard Business School Press, 2005.

Brown, John Seely, and Paul Duguid. *The Social Life of Information.* Boston: Harvard Business School Press, 2000.

Buckingham, Marcus, and Curt Coffman. *First Break All The Rules: What the World's Greatest Managers Do Differently.* New York: Simon & Schuster, 1999.

Conger, Jay Alden. *Learning to Lead: The Art of Transforming Managers into Leaders.* San Francisco: Jossey-Bass, 1992.

Crossland, Ron, and Gregg Thompson. *The Leadership Experience: From Individual Success to Organizational Significance.* New York: Select Books, 2007.

Damasio, Antonio. *Descartes' Error: Emotion, Reason, and the Human Brain.* New York: Grosset/Putnam, 1994.

Looking for Spinoza: Joy, Sorrow, and the Feeling Brain. Orlando, FL: Harcourt, 2003.

The Feeling of What Happens: Body and Emotion in the Making of Consciousness. New York: Harcourt Brace, 1999.

DeLoache, Judy S. "Mindful of Symbols." *Scientific American,* July 2005.

Farson, Richard. *Management of the Absurd: Paradoxes in Leadership.* New York: Touchstone, 1997.

Fernández-Aráoz, Claudio. "Getting the Right People at the Top." *Sloan Management Review* 46, no. 4 (summer 2005).

Fu, Ping Ping, et al. "The Impact of Societal Cultural Values and Individual

Social Beliefs on the Perceived Effectiveness of Managerial Influence Strategies." *Journal of International Business Studies* 35, no. 4 (July 2004).

Gardner, Howard. *Changing Minds: The Art and Science of Changing Our Own and Other People's Minds.* Boston: Harvard Business School Press, 2004.

Leading Minds: An Anatomy of Leadership. New York: Basic Books, 1995.

Gardner, John W. *Self-Renewal: The Individual and the Innovative Society.* New York: W. W. Norton, 1981.

Gibson, Cristina B., and Mary E. Zellmer-Bruhn. "Metaphors and Meaning: An Intercultural Analysis of the Concept of Teamwork." *Administrative Science Quarterly,* July 2001.

Glaser, Judith E. *The DNA of Leadership: Leverage Your Instincts to Communicate-Differentiate-Innovate.* Avon, MA: Platinum Press, 2006.

Goleman, Daniel, Richard Boyatzis, and Annie McKee. "Primal Leadership: The Hidden Driver of Great Performance." *Harvard Business Review* 79, no. 11 (December 2001).

Gregersen, Hal B., Allen J. Morrison, and J. Stewart Black. "Developing Leaders for the Global Frontier." *Sloan Management Review* 40, no. 1 (Fall 1998).

Hall-Jamieson, Kathleen. *Eloquence in an Electronic Age: The Transformation of Political Speechmaking.* New York: Oxford University Press, 1990.

Heath, Chip, and Dan Heath. *Made to Stick: Why Some Ideas Survive and Others Die.* New York: Random House, 2007.

Hogarth, Robin. *Educating Intuition.* Chicago: University of Chicago Press, 2001.

Jackson, Brooks, and Kathleen Hall-Jamieson. *UnSpun: Finding Facts in a World of Disinformation.* New York: Random House, 2007.

Johnson, Steven. *Mind Wide Open: Your Brain and the Neuroscience of Everyday Life.* New York: Scribner, 2004.

Kets de Vries, Manfred. *The Leadership Mystique: A User's Manual for the Human Enterprise.* London: Financial Times/Prentice Hall, 2001.

Koestenbaum, Peter. *Leadership: The Innerside of Greatness; A Philosophy for Leaders.* San Francisco: Jossey-Bass, 2002.

Kramer, Roderick M. "Trust and Distrust in Organizations: Emerging Perspective, Enduring Questions." *Annual Review of Psychology* 50 (1999).

Lakoff, George, and Mark Johnson. *Metaphors We Live By.* Chicago: University of Chicago Press, 1980.

Lazarus, Richard S., and Bernice N. Lazarus. *Passion and Reason: Making Sense of Our Emotions*. New York: Oxford University Press, 1996.

Learning International. "Strategic Vision: A New Role for Corporate Leaders." Stamford, CT: Learning International, Inc., 1986.

LeDoux, Joseph. *The Emotional Brain: The Mysterious Underpinnings of Emotional Life*. New York: Touchstone, 1996.

Lopez, Barry. *Crossing Open Ground*. New York: Vintage Books, 1989.

Lumet, Sidney. *Making Movies*. New York: Vintage Books, 1996.

Manusov, Valerie, and Miles L. Patterson. *The Sage Handbook of Nonverbal Communication*. Thousand Oaks, CA: Sage Publications, 2006.

Maslow, Abraham. *Toward a Psychology of Being*. Princeton, NJ: Van Nostrand, 1968.

Mayer, J. D., D. Goleman, D. Barrett, et al. "Leading by Feel." *Harvard Business Review* 82, no. 1 (January 2004).

McKee, Robert. "Storytelling That Moves People." *Harvard Business Review* 81, no. 6 (June 2003).

Mithen, Steven J. *The Prehistory of the Mind: The Cognitive Origins of Art, Religion, and Science*. London: Thames and Hudson, 1996.

"New Research Shows Executives Lack the 'Gift of Gab,'" *Online Recruitment*, October 12, 2003. http://www.onrec.com/content2/ news.asp?ID=3316.

"Only One-Third of Companies Say Their Employees Understand and Live Business Strategy in Daily Jobs." *International Association of Business Communicators*, September 13, 2005. http://news.iabc.com/ index.php?s=press_releases&item=19.

O'Toole, Kathleen. "What Makes Some Ideas Hang Around." *Stanford Business* 70, no. 2 (February 2002).

Oyama, Susan. *Evolution's Eye: A Systems View of the Biology-Culture Divide*. Durham, NC: Duke University Press, 2000.

Paulos, John Allen. *A Mathematician Reads the Newspaper*. New York: Basic Books, 1995.

Pinker, Steven. *How the Mind Works*. New York: W. W. Norton, 1996.

Price, Harrison "Buzz." Walt's Revolution! By the Numbers. Orlando, FL: Ripley Entertainment, 2004.

Ramachandran, V. S. *A Brief Tour of Human Consciousness: From Imposter Poodles to Purple Numbers*. New York: Pi Press, 2004.

Ratey, John H. *A User's Guide to the Brain: Perception, Attention, and the Four Theaters of the Brain*. New York: Vintage, 2002.

Ready, Douglas A. "How Storytelling Builds Next-Generation Leaders." *Sloan Management Review* 43, no. 4 (Summer 2002).

Ridley, Matt. *Nature Via Nurture: Genes, Experience, and What Makes Us Human.* New York: HarperCollins, 2003.

Rosenberg, Scott. "The Data Artist." Salon.com, March 10, 1997. http://www.salon.com/march97/tufte2970310.html.

Sachs, Jessica Snyder. "A Spielberg in Your Own Mind." *Popular Science,* July 2003.

Sacks, Oliver. *The Man Who Mistook His Wife for a Hat: and Other Clinical Tales.* New York: HarperPerennial, 1970.

Schwartz, Peter. *The Art of the Long View: Planning for the Future in an Uncertain World.* New York: Doubleday, 1996.

"Seven Common Leadership Complaints from CEOs." *Chief Learning Officer,* October 2007. http://www.clomedia.com/in-the-news/2007/October/1971/index.php.

Shaffer, Jim. *The Leadership Solution.* New York: McGraw Hill, 2000.

Siegel, Daniel J. *The Developing Mind: How Relationships and the Brain Interact to Shape Who We Are.* New York: Guilford Press, 1999.

Smith, Georgianne. "Emotional, Symbolic, and Factual Dimensions of Leadership Communication." Unpublished dissertation. Pepperdine University, August 1977.

Sull, Donald N., and Charles Spinosa. "Promise-Based Management: The Essence of Execution." *Harvard Business Review* 85, no. 4 (April 2007).

Tattersall, Ian. "Drenched in Symbolism." *Scientific American* 281, no. 1 (July 2003).

Winchester, James A. "The Effect of Symbolic and Factual Content on Leader Communications." Unpublished dissertation. Pepperdine University, August 1997.

ABOUT THE AUTHOR

Ron Crossland is a four-time entrepreneur with a three wins and one loss track record. He earned a BS in Electronics Engineering Technology, but considers himself a recovering engineer. He earned an MBA with an emphasis in organizational behavior, but now works solo from his cubicle at home by the backdoor. Ron is Chairman of Bluepoint Leadership Development and a Managing Director for Tom Peters Group, Ltd. He lives in Mason, Ohio with his wife and two sons.

INDEX